EFFECTIVE E-MARKETING STRATEGIES

Proven Online Marketing Tactics
Designed to Increase Profit and Move your
Business Ahead of the Competition

Curtis Carmichael

Published by HyperFusion, LLC., Milford, New Hampshire.

Category: Business / Internet Marketing

ISBN-13: 978-1482767377
ISBN-10: 1482767376

DEDICATION

To Rachael, for her support and encouragement in helping me write this book.

To my father and brother who have always encouraged me to write, and the rest of my family for their support and feedback.

And to everyone else in their pursuit of true financial freedom and the 'American Dream': I wish you the very best and hope this book helps you along the way.

TABLE OF CONTENTS

··· **❶** ···
FOREWORD AND INTRODUCTION

If you are like me, you never seem to fall short of ideas for a new product or service either online or in the 'real world.' You may have started a business or started building a product or service in the past but perhaps due to a lack of personal experience, time, financial or human resources had to put the idea on hold. Perhaps you also may have experienced associated challenges as a one-person operation or conflicts in a multi-person team. Or, the idea presented legal challenges and was deemed too risky to bring to market. Perhaps it had to be shelved due to perceived low profit margins associated with high maintenance costs, etc.

Many times, startups tend to fail but with the right strategy, people, connections, experience, funding and tools, you can defy the odds and build a successful company. The Internet still offers many great opportunities, despite large companies having claimed key areas. For example:

- Google with search
- eBay for auctions
- Flickr for photo uploads
- Craigslist for classifieds
- LinkedIn for professional networking
- Groupon and Living Social for daily deals
- Facebook for personal social networking

The trick is to define niches rather than focusing on the masses (i.e. a photo sharing site for outdoor enthusiasts) or you can combine features from the more popular sites (i.e. the best of Facebook + LinkedIn), while perhaps still focusing on building a niche site with community aspects. It could also be something relatively simple but useful, such as a lost and found web site or application that you believe could gain popularity through word of mouth and news outlets. Other entrepreneurs have cloned a concept and introduced it to another world region. For instance, a Pinterest clone was created called Pinspire which was heavily marketed outside North America and quickly grew in popularity. The Samwer Brothers out of Germany are well known for their success with this model (Wauters, 2011). Many large companies are buying out clones, which lines the pockets of entrepreneurs and benefits the dominant company as it increased their market share for typically less money over what it would have cost them when they could not immediately capitalize on the opportunity in other areas of the world. Some companies buy comparable companies or organizations that could otherwise merge nicely with their product or service to quickly introduce more features to their customers and acquire talent. The result is typically a win-win. Still, opportunities exist where you do not need to focus in niche areas but they are rare.

NOT EVERYTHING HAS BEEN INVENTED

As the saying goes, if you thought of an idea, someone else likely has. Or, everything has essentially already been invented (i.e. the auto steering wheel, etc.) and most inventions stem from those core concepts. There is some truth to this, but if you can identify the next best thing, you will be very wealthy. The Internet was largely ignored when it first became available to anyone who wanted to subscribe to it – aside from it being somewhat expensive, people generally could not identify with it or see how it could benefit them. The early investors saw this as the next big 'gold rush' however and were right on. With the absence of too much competition, their products became the go-to site and they quickly grew in popularity. Many people became millionaires in the so-called dot com boom. Business opportunities aside, I always joke I should have registered generic dictionary words as .com's back then in light of their $1M+ values today.

Some view mobile phones as the newest focus territory. Smartphones are growing considerably popular in the USA, Canada and UK. They are also becoming more popular in less developed countries as phones are generally cheaper over PCs/laptops and wireless phone service costing less over satellite and high-speed Internet. This means there is a largely untapped business opportunity for the latter. If a new application or mobile site is introduced for this growing population and translated for their native languages, it can be viewed as the 'go to' site for X,Y,Z and help the company become the dominant player in this region while creating new jobs and help improve the economy. Controversially, in English speaking parts of the world where smartphones are quite popular, a large opportunity still exists for a developer to create a popular mobile app/game which can quickly convert to significant profit. Angry Birds, Fruit Ninja and others were a huge success. If you were able to create a similar application and sold it for $2.99 let's say, multiply that by 500,000 users (on the low side but to throw out a number), that would gross $1,495,000. Remember, two major mobile markets exist – Google's Android Market for Android devices and Apple's mobile market, so the grossed amount would likely be double this gross amount. You could also be successful in offering a free version of the application supported by small, out of the way advertisements. Both versions would be popular as some people prefer paying a small price to not see advertisements and there are also people who do not want to buy an application. The Internet helped build the mentality and for some people an expectation that all content should be free so you want to cater to both crowds. After all, bottom line, you are looking to increase downloads to help spread the popularity/word of mouth and both options still add to the bottom line. (A side note: ~$3M may not seem like a significant gross to larger companies but it is a significant amount for independent developers and is valuable in leveraging any other games introduced.)

POWERFUL WEB TOOLS ABOUND FOR ENTREPRENEURS

One of the great things about the Internet is that it empowers independent entrepreneurs and small teams to use free, enterprise-ready open source tools to build powerful web applications. Or, one can simply purchase a clone or 'turn-key' script (i.e. a script from the PHP script library at HotScripts.com) and either prototype or take a concept to market very quickly. Drupal, WordPress, Joomla and DotNetNuke are very popular open source CMS programs that let developers easily add to the core program functionality via plugins and modules. Third party themes/frameworks can further extend functionality while creating a professional looking web site for a small investment, which you can easily modify within the CMS' web-based administration area to more closely match your business' requirements and brand. Responsive and fluid web design principles tend to be built-in to many themes offered today which is a significant time saver over programming the responses and design patterns yourself. ThemeForest.com is a great resource for professionally designed themes and the site's network provides access to stock photography, web site components and other resources you can use to enhance your site.

Not to digress from the overview focus in this chapter too much, but if you do want to use a theme/framework for your site, try to find one that:

- Is GPL or MIT licensed.
- Offers 100% open source code to streamline code edits if necessary (and prevent potential hassles getting your site to work with Zend or IonCube encoders).
- Allows you to use the theme on multiple domain names/sites.
- Free lifetime updates and at least lifetime email/forum-based tech support is optimal for the most flexibility.

You may not get all of these so sometimes it comes down to a cost/benefit analysis (i.e. you being OK paying for updates after X months, paying for support, paying extra to install and use the code base with multiple domains, sites, etc.

PASSION AND AUTOMATION ARE KEY

The goal in identifying what you want to build should always revolve around whether it is something you are truly passionate about and if you have any others on your team, whether they are truly interested in the idea and can share the same entrepreneurial spirit as you. In addition, equally important is the idea preferably should be one that can be automated as much as possible to run on its own after you/your team invests the time and money in building the product. The automation aspect allows you step back a bit, take a real vacation for once (joking) and ultimately start other ventures if desired. Preferably, you want to diversify your product portfolio, in the event a larger, more powerful company convinces people to use their product over yours and discourages advertisers to continue doing business with you. Similarly, if you sell an idea, understanding the entrepreneurial mindset, you likely want to continue having your own business to have the freedom to model your own products and market them against your own strategic goals and objectives so you would have other products you can continue working on after (provided the sale agreement does not call for too much of your time with the transition/hand-off effort).

Some business models having a near 100% automation aspect (beyond an occasional marketing push) include:

A PROFESSIONAL DIRECTORY SITE

For instance a directory of dentists in the USA. An initial collection/data entry effort creates the directory and lists most dentists at the premium level for a specified trial period (i.e. 30-90 days), after which they would be downgraded to the free level with limited listing features. An email marketing campaign could help push dentists to upgrade their listing for X amount, good for Y days. The levels might be bronze, silver, gold and platinum with varying listing features. The benefit to the dentist would be they would appear above their competition with premium list options, it is a valuable piece of their overall business promotional effort to help get the word out in as many places and the directory itself has great SEO/ranking in Google, etc. (if accurate).

ELECTRONIC MEDIA/PUBLICATIONS

Create an electronic product (i.e. sound clip, theme for a popular CMS, template, ebook, etc.) and after the initial period you invest in the product, you can automate the entire sales process by uploading the files with a service such as e-junkie.com. You advertise the product on the web such as via an email marketing campaign and optimized landing pages, affiliate program, etc. and people can instantly purchase the product via PayPal or other system and receive an email minutes later with a download link. You have no physical inventory to manage and your income accumulates in the background within PayPal, which you can transfer to your bank account or request a check.

TRAINING PROGRAMS

You may want to consult/partner with someone well-known in the industry to build a solid reputation behind the training program and have it deemed to have any significant authoritative value. You would work closely with the thought leader to develop a program, perhaps work out a deal to cut the profit 50/50 and input the training material in a training program such as Questionmark. You can setup a series of modules/classes for the person to word towards certification, charging them X amount for each one, or for the certification program all together. Alternatively, you can setup a subscription-based learning resource where new, valuable material is guaranteed to be introduced every day or week and charge for access to that. Perhaps offer a $1 trial for X days and then encourage the use to sign up for the whole year at a cost savings to capture more revenue up front which looks better on sales report.

AUTO BLOGGING

If you create a site in WordPress for instance (the actual version you can download and install on your own server is recommended, for flexibility), you can install plugins/modules that can pull in content from RSS feeds and syndicated sources to automatically fill your web site up with valuable, current news, photos and video (i.e. WP Robot, FeedWordPress, etc.) The trick for success with this is to research what might be a good niche for the site's focus. You want to avoid focusing on competitive subjects such as health care, world news, politics, etc. unless you are very passionate in one area and would like to try a concept out. (Just make sure you do the keyword research ahead of time, via Google's Keyword Suggestion Tool and other resources and review some of the top ranked sites/blogs to see what they are doing as part of your analysis.) If you install WordPress as a network site (formerly known as WordPress MU), you only need to invest in installing the plugins, themes, etc. once and you can easily setup a new site within that framework for another niche area on another SEO-optimized domain name with minimal time investment. You would make money with contextual ad networks such as Google AdSense, which pay you every time someone clicks on a relevant text or graphic/video ad that gets displayed on your site (you only need to place a small code snippet to have these ads automatically appear). AdBrite, AdRoll, Text-Link-Ads.com and Kontera are other popular solutions that pay you every time someone clicks on an ad displayed from their network (some programs limit participation and require certain criteria such as X number of visitors in Y time, etc.) Other programs exist for high traffic sites that pay you based on cost per impression which can be automated as well. Sometimes however, you may realize a higher profit if you run your own ad program with perhaps Google's DoubleClick system or OpenX as niche sites can command a higher than average CPM (cost per 1,000 impressions). You might also want to consider reducing the amount of automation to introduce some original content to further increase your rankings in Google and other search engines. If you write a lot of original content while keeping the reader in mind (so they find value in it and return/share it with others), that can help increase readership and SEO. You can potentially get your site indexed in Google News if you add contract editors down the road (Google requires more than one blogger/editor behind a site to get listed).

WEB HOSTING SERVICE

You can run your own web site hosting company using turn-key software packages. You can configure these to sell unused space on your web hosting account (if your web hosting provider allows this), or you could setup a model similar to what Intuit web site builder does for small companies that want a professional low cost web site quickly and charge for hosting, in addition to features.

AFFILIATE/DROP-SHIP PROGRAMS

You can either feature individual products on your web site using products/images from the affiliate (i.e. from Commission Junction or ClickBank), or you could embed a virtual store on your site similar to what Amazon offers with their aStore implementation. Alternatively, you can use an affiliate storefront script available at HotScripts.com that interfaces with Amazon and ClickBank (the latter for digital products), or subscribe to Amazon's web store service that lets you fill the store with their products. Automated drop shipping via a third party storefront is made possible with Shopster (www.shopster.com) which runs on its own after some time setting it up.

WHITE LABEL PROGRAMS

If you wanted a low-investment way to partner with leading services while making it seem as if it was your own product, white label programs are an excellent option. For instance, there are many white label options from email service providers (i.e. ExactTarget) and options for doing the same for online storage/backup applications and cloud-based SMS marketing utilities. A popular white label program is offered by GoDaddy where they allow companies and individuals to serve as quasi-affiliates under the guise of their own branded domain name registration site. Another (through CafePress.com) lets you create your own branded apparel store, featuring your own designs and products selected from their inventory. You can send people to these web sites using various e-marketing strategies described in this book and many allow you to mark up base prices to your own price where you collect the difference.

Caveat: While these scenarios may be very close to being fully automated, nothing is truly 100% automated after you launch the product/service. It can be, and by saying this, you imply you would be kicking back and letting the site run on its own and perhaps only checking in on the site from time to time to review performance. In doing this however, you run the risk of the competition building something 'bigger and better' or consumers/business clients losing interest in the web site, resulting with a potential loss of income. A semi-automated site, if built right should not require too much time maintaining it after launch but still requires new content, a redesign every so often (perhaps at least once a year, so long as it does not significantly take away from the user interface/experience your visitors are used to), removing duplicate entries from automated content pushes, cleaning stray comment spam that passed through a filter, editing comments, marketing your site, etc.

An aside: Turn-key web site software can work great but if you want a successful web site, even if you launch on a 'phase one' approach or alpha/beta milestone, the site needs to work great and not have any software glitches. Furthermore, the site needs to have a great user interface (design/layout customizations) and the user experience/flow should work flawlessly. If you overlook these, your site may receive negative word of mouth/reviews and no one will want to return, essentially wasting any time/resources you spent on marketing and building the site. You also want to attract editors/publications so they write about your product, giving you free publicity.

SUCCESS IN BUSINESS

"Success = ambition + vision + execution + persistence + luck + timing; with the first four being things you can control and the last two being externalities that you cannot."
(Karbasfrooshan, 2012)

When you finish reading this and work on your idea/venture, if there is one important concept to take away from this book that is to never, never give up. It is OK to 'shelf' an idea to pick up later on but never abandon it – unless the cost/benefit outlooks changes, then it might make sense. As many successful entrepreneurs say, "success = failure squared" so it is not out of the ordinary to fail many times over with a concept or different ideas (on the contrary, some degree of 'failure' is to be expected as your first attempt(s) statistically will require some refinement). Eventually, you will perfect the idea or will find the right concept that really takes off. Sometimes it is just the wrong time to pursue something, other times it just needs refinement to be different, or other times it needs more resources (monetary and people) to market and take off.

Starting a business is not easy. Successful entrepreneurs need to understand that to be successful, their business becomes their life (symbolically and in actuality at times.) If a business owner invests roughly 1-2 hours every day towards their business, at least 4-5 days of the week, their rate of probable success increases significantly.

On a personal note, here are a few Internet ventures I started on my own that I would consider failures and what I learned:

- **BottleBid.com**
  An online auction site for antique bottle collectors (with a satellite sites, BottleAuction.com and BottleAuctions.com). Unfortunately, most dealers and collectors still preferred eBay due to the high traffic and regularly updated inventory.
- **CoinSniper.com**
  An online auction site for coin collectors. Same deal with BottleBid.com (eBay essentially owned/controlled the auction environment and niche auction sites had little true market share in comparison to this giant).
- **PicSharing.com**
  An online photo-sharing web site. At the time, Kodak PhotoNet was the major player and I found it difficult to gain appropriate traction to have a true competitive edge in this area.
- **Trendport**
  An online shopping site for clothing/apparel and fashion accessories. Clothing is among the most competitive areas on the Internet and as a one-person operation with limited resources at the time, was unable to carry this too far. However, I do not view this as a complete failure. This concept still has potential, perhaps as niche Pinterest clone that could generate a good source of income via contextual ads, affiliate ads, etc.

I still do not consider these failures. I have since sold the CoinSniper.com and PicSharing.com domain names but there is always room to grow the concepts and add other components to them to make them more attractive and competitive. In the end, it comes down to reviewing all of your ideas, doing a cost/benefit analysis, selecting what you feel your best idea is and focusing on that.

You should also do some market research to understand your audience, technological barriers, etc. before moving with an idea. comScore (www.comscore.com) has some great resources you can subscribe to, as do a number of other sites that focus exclusively on your market segment/niche.

SOURCE OF MOTIVATION

"Genius is one percent inspiration and
ninety-nine percent perspiration."
– Thomas A. Edison

You will likely become discouraged at all stages of creating/growing your site. The planning stage requires a good amount of work alone, and building the site, many long days/nights and at times, weekends. This is normal and you are not alone. Thomas A. Edison could not have said this any better, reflecting on his quote at the beginning of this section. He is also known for another popular quote worth noting: "I have not failed. I've just found 10,000 ways that won't work."

As you plan or build your site, some items that might help your push may be:

- **Work with a mentor that has demonstrated success in your focus area to help guide you through challenges.** As the saying goes, success comes to those who associate and exchange ideas with other successful people. They can offer valuable feedback, advice and guidance. Perhaps see if they may be available on a consulting basis or offer a percentage of profit to have them come on board as a partner.
- **Join a local industry user group, entrepreneur group or industry association for free or low-cost guidance.** Many

associations have large annual meet-ups and various small meet-ups throughout the year with an online listserv/mailing list.

- **Purchase audio CDs and books on the subject** – or even material that does not specifically focus on what you are doing but to help encourage success from a spiritual/general motivation perspective (i.e. the negative push/drive – perhaps attributed to a current job you do not enjoy, financial stress/debt, etc.) I found quote books to be valuable as well. Perhaps buy a motivational poster to place above your computer desk.

- **Somewhat humorous, but effective: drive by large lake and ocean-front houses/mansions.** If you are after the American dream, this can encourage you there is light at the end of the tunnel and you could live like them.

- **Watch infomercials** – I learned some core marketing/sales concepts from these. Albeit, I did find many of them to be corny but they are successful sales pitches funded by multi-million dollar companies.

- **See what other people are doing to market their web sites online.** Also worthwhile to review landing pages and the sales flow/strategy involved with them. If the landing page features a video, listen closely and place yourself in the presenter's shoes and think about why he/she is saying to attract the sale.

- **Do not be afraid to attend a Multi-Level Marketing (MLM) seminar/conference.** Listen and watch carefully as every minute is a carefully rehearsed presentation – in this instance, based on thousands of $$ spent on researching how to effectively sell to people wanting to 'beat the system' and achieve financial freedom. Again, concentrate on the message and placing yourself in the sales team's shoes and you can walk away with valuable insight – also taking into consideration the marketing materials/methods used to get the people to the conference. In my opinion, these MLM pitches are stacked against the consumer as the event host reportedly makes all their money on paid seminars and learning materials such as CDs, books, etc.

BEFORE WE BEGIN...

This book assumes you have a solid basic understanding of computers (Windows or Mac) and how the Internet works. It is also beneficial if you have had some University-level course exposure (or having read an in-depth book) to/on economics, marketing and some entry-level 'real world' experience in any area of web design, development or online marketing. The latter is not absolutely necessary but serves as a nice foundation in developing your business. If you have attempted one or more businesses/ventures in the past, that is fine as well as you know what has worked and what has not worked so well and you can gain/grow from this valuable experience. More importantly, in any case is the will/drive to succeed and your ability to pace steady progress towards developing your business.

All suggestions in this book assume you are starting a new business in the USA but the material is also useful if you wish to refine/restructure an existing business and you can certainly apply most of everything in this book in other areas of the world as well.

I will review many of the popular and fundamental e-marketing trends, strategies and tactics used by professional Internet marketers in today's market but the scope of this book is being limited to delivering more of an overview, versus an in-depth 'how-to' do X, Y and Z. This is because marketing tools often change to adapt improved user interfaces and experiences, software companies merging together which consolidates features, etc. so identifying all of the ways to address a particular task with a specific software program may change in the next few months but the spirit of what is being done typically will not. In addition, the depth and involvement of e-marketing specialties is so vast that documenting a complete scope for each one could potentially take years to complete. To shed some light on this, full-time specialty roles have materialized in the past few years that focus exclusively on areas such as e-mail marketing, web site analytics, etc. and some of these areas can be further broken down into sub-specialty areas. Google is a great resource to find the latest trends/information as are vendor web sites, industry forums/publications, etc.

··· ❷ ···
PROJECT MANAGEMENT

As you build your online marketing presence, to prevent things from 'falling through the cracks,' you might want to take a look at formal project management utilities to help manage day-to-day tasks and 'big-picture' items between multiple brands. A formal system, after adjusting to a small learning curve and work process change, helps virtually anyone to keep focused and stay on task to ensure deliverables are presented on-time and in-budget. A simple spreadsheet-based solution can work for budget-strapped organizations as well.

Google Calendar is a great tool to use for managing your email marketing efforts. This is described in more detail in the email marketing chapter.

Excel, OpenOffice.org Calc or even a Google Docs Spreadsheet are good basic project management tools. At a previous company, I maintained a Google Docs spreadsheet and shared this with various departments to keep everyone in the loop/informed on progress, priorities, etc. with email follow-ups and face to face catch-up and project review sessions to help manage multiple projects as a one-person Internet marketing and web development department. Although a simple and low-cost tool/process, it greatly helped keep the lines of communication open and streamlined management.

The spreadsheet solution can work if you keep it up-to-date often as it can be challenging at times if more than one project management tool is being used (with outside vendors for example). If you use the spreadsheet method, some key columns you may want to consider including are:

- Product/Brand
- Requester

- Stakeholder/product owner
- Date requested
- Due date (desired)
- Due date (drop dead)
- Brief description of request followed by note on where to go to/reference more detail
- Priority level (1-5, 1 most pressing, 5 not urgent) followed by sub priority level (A, B, C). Example: 1A.
- Notes - progress made, waiting on/holding pattern and why/on who?
- Estimated # of hours (original)
- # of hours remaining (estimated)

If you have a large flow of incoming projects and many existing requests to fulfill, it may make sense to subscribe to a commercial project management solution such as Basecamp. Basecamp is becoming a popular project management tool hosted on the cloud that reduces the amount of manual entry involved and allows others to input new requests in the system and edit existing requests to modify priorities, etc. (huge time saver). The only challenge is sometimes winning support from the team as this new method may be difficult to enforce as some product owners may prefer continuing to email new requests to you (OK every once in a while but if you receive lots of requests, the benefit of this new system may not be fully realized as it still requires manual entry, etc. from you, while incurring the additional on-going service charge.) If this becomes difficult to manage, you might want to consider an alternate possibility involving some sort of email-based/initiated ticket system such as Zendesk (www.zendesk.com). A product owner can send a new request to an email address you provide them with to create a new ticket and someone can quickly login and assign the ticket to someone and/or enter/modify request details.

Many project management systems can help you manage

communication with stakeholders by optionally auto-sending them an email if a ticket/project has been closed/completed or for simple modifications (i.e. reducing the ETA, etc.) This can potentially send many emails so in many cases (depending on the software used), you can turn this feature off if desired but in my opinion, it does not hurt to over-communicate unless someone prefers they do not receive the e-mail based updates.

If you develop software and you are looking for something a bit more advanced/specific for your field, Atlassian JIRA is an excellent comprehensive project management/reporting product that should meet all your requirements. In addition, a site called Planning Poker (www.planningpoker.com) works great for team project estimation meetings/exercises and is widely used by agile/scrum organizations.

As an aside, if your team or organization has less than 10 people and some of your colleagues work off-site/remote, Google+ Hangouts is a great free tool to do face-to-face 'stand-ups' or quick catch-up sessions. Google+ Hangouts Extended lets you share your screen with others (www.join.me is also another great screen share alternative). If you have more than 10 members on your team, WebEx's various web conferencing solutions or Adobe Acrobat Connect have been known to serve this requirement well. The only possible draw-back is the latter two options may require the user to install software on their computer (which may not be possible if their IT department prevents this, or possible compatibility conflict may arise).

If you work with many clients (internal and/or external), or manage a number of calls with prospective clients, a few popular automatic scheduling programs you might find valuable are:

- TimeBridge - www.timebridge.com (also at www.meetwith.me)
- Setster - www.setster.com
- TimeCenter - www.timecenter.com

- TimeTrade - www.timetrade.com
- Appointron - www.appointron.com
- BookFresh - www.bookfresh.com
- BookedIN - www.getbookedin.com
- Genbook - www.genbook.com
- Doodle - www.doodle.com

Many of these tools are free but the paid versions might offer enhanced features or cater to enterprise companies a bit more. They generally all have one purpose in mind – to allow someone to view your calendar/availability and schedule a phone call/in-person meeting, preventing 'schedule tag.' You availability is determined from calendars you sync with the program and any exceptions you add.

One important piece to consider with project management which goes without saying for most people, treat internal and external customers as equals and as if they are all your boss. With excellent service come great results, especially when you can deliver on all your promises and deadlines. Equally important is that all team members believe and subscribe to this concept.

REGISTERING A DOMAIN NAME

If you need a domain name for your business, personal business venture or you want to invest in a domain name for a future entrepreneurial venture or other purpose, there are a number of items you should consider.

First, you will want to make sure your domain name is memorable and high-impact. Try to stay away with including hyphens in your domain or numbers as this decreases the value of your domain and makes it increasingly difficult for your customers to recall. Also, although domain names can be up to 256 characters in length, long domain names have like consequences and reduces the likeliness of your customers to type in the domain into their web browser if they didn't find you on the web and could otherwise click on a link.

Try to secure all top level domain (TLDs) suffixes such as .com, .net and .org for your business, especially if you believe you have a solid business idea. Your competitors might try to grab alternate domain name suffixes or you might have unscrupulous 'investors' who see your business thrive, register the names and then try to 'blackmail' you in a sense by refusing to transfer the name to you without paying a large sum – in the past these people have even gone so far as to setup a placeholder page or small site with pornography, leftist or far-right political messages, etc. to try to leverage their goals in this end. If you own a trademark (and I suggest you at least register your trademark on the state level, if not a federal trademark through the USPTO) – you have some legal recourse through intellectual property (IP) lawyers and perhaps the domain's registrar such as GoDaddy's legal department or the Internet Corporation for Assigned Names and Numbers (ICANN) can provide you with some assistance as they are the governing body for all registrars.

To search for a domain name, go to a domain registrar's web site to see if it is available. You can go to other domain search sites but there is no saying on whether available names are flagged by these sites - an alert mechanism in other words - that lets the Webmaster know a top quality domain is up for grabs. That's why I tend to always do domain research on a major domain registration web site such as GoDaddy.com because I doubt they have such a mechanism in place and even if they did, their business plan requires them to focus on other areas so there would be very limited resources situated for this endeavor... and they would also be bound to ICANN's rules and regulations which may actually prevent them from doing this. Slight tangent... but an important item to get across as I have had a few excellent available domains 'stolen' from me when I did not act fast enough to register them while researching on smaller domain name availability checker sites and/or WHOIS tools.

When searching for a domain, you might want to pull up the following web sites to assist with your search:

- **The U.S. Patent and Trademark Office (USPTO)** web site at www.uspto.gov to determine if a name is registered as a trademark, to avoid a potential legal dispute down the road (suggest you query plurals, hyphens, spaces, etc. where appropriate and like-sounding names).
- **Thesaurus.com** – because most likely your domain name is taken, but you can use this site to help generate similar words to generate a new creative trademark/domain name. GoDaddy's domain name search area lists suggestions for you as well but the best alternatives generally would come from you vs. an automated suggestion system for alternatives.
- **Google.com** (or similar search engine) – suggest you use this to query words associated with your domain name to determine popularity, possible trademark infringement not

found through USPTO's tool – if someone didn't register their mark with the federal registrar, etc.)

If you plan on registering a large amount of domain names (and registering names can be quite addictive to some), GoDaddy.com offers a Domain Discount Club where you pay X amount for a subscription allowing you to take advantage of "rock bottom" prices for new domain name registrations and renewals for many domain suffixes. Suggest you weigh pros and cons subscribing to this service however because it may only make sense if you plan on maintaining ~100 domain names/year or so. Coupon and promo code sites such as FatWallet.com are good to take a look at as well to weigh all options. FatWallet.com maintains GoDaddy promo codes at www.fatwallet.com/godaddy-coupons and you may be able to find a few others via a Google search for "GoDaddy promo".

A few other domain tools you may wish to explore can be found at www.domaintools.com. Their WHOIS tool specifies whether a domain name has been registered before, based upon their historical WHOIS information.

A few of the most popular domain name registrars:

- GoDaddy – www.godaddy.com
- Moniker - www.moniker.com
- NameCheap - www.namecheap.com
- eNom - www.enom.com
- Register.com - www.register.com

DOMAIN NAME PARKING – IN A NUTSHELL

As you build your domain name portfolio, you may not have time to build a web site for all of them at once. As such, rather than have the domains remain in an 'idle' state and not collect any revenue, domain name parking offers a way for you to jumpstart your site's SEO while collecting revenue from third-party ads.

These days, domain name parking services are abound – a quick Google search indicates 5-10 popular services and many other web sites offering the service. Upon further research (and my own experience), I determined not many people have luck parking their domain names with a service. Others, and myself are lucky to get more than 25-50 cents per day. And I have over 100 domain names. Not to complain because the earnings definitely rival most US-based savings accounts but one can do better and the cost/benefit doesn't weigh out with each domain name costing somewhere in the range of $7-10 USD.

Of all the services, you'll have the most luck with one allowing you to optimize the content/ads displayed on your domains. Traditionally, the most successful domains are B2B related so you'll want to concentrate on these ones as they will pay out better – in most cases, again, with my own experience and reading feedback from others on domain parking. Some of the best domain parking services are:

- GoDaddy's domain parking service - www.godaddy.com/gdshop/park/landing.asp
- RevenueDirect.com – www.revenuedirect.com
- Google's domain parking service - www.google.com/domainpark
- Sedo.com – www.sedo.com
- SEOparking.com – www.seoparking.com

The latter is setup in an interesting format – it takes more time to setup the domains but the end result allows you to display blog entries of your choosing on your web site on a WordPress blog. Clever format but as a rule of thumb, I always like to have original content on my web site. WordPress blogs do have excellent SEO capabilities however, as long as you don't abuse SEO principles, etc.

If you want to consider running your own domain parking service you might want to take a look at a program called Domain Trader (www.smartscript.net/domaintrader). Looks like a great program but you'll want to take a good look at this before moving ahead and purchasing. I haven't used it because I'm not sure if the $$ income benefits would be worth the investment based on my experience in this area. Some of the sites the software developer mentions no longer appear to be active as well, for what it's worth. You might be able to find a few other 'out of the box' programs available on the web and another option might be to develop your own system, perhaps just to serve your own domains on your server or virtual host account.

NamePros.com is an excellent resource where people who are in the business of domain name parking share ideas and feedback. If you are new to this area, you may find posting forum inquiries on the site beneficial. The Lazy Domainer (www.thelazydomainer.com) is another good resource but is setup in 'infomercial' format – does have some nice information however.

Pending review/approval from your legal department (or sole legal advisor), if you do not use your domain names presently, I strongly suggest you consider domain parking options. If you don't your domain registrar tends to collect 100% from ads displayed on your temporary parked page by default (if applicable, but usually the case with GoDaddy for instance, at the time of this writing). You may or may not collect big $$ from this, but it will at least help you gauge which domains might be worth developing first based on pageviews, ad clicks, etc. your domain parking service you partner with may report.

I personally park my domains with RevenueDirect.com not necessarily because of the payouts (it is about the same as others*) but because of the vast amount of reporting available. My thought process is in the time being, rather than have my domains not pull in any $$ at all, I'd at least be making some money – as Ben Franklin was famously quoted as saying, "a penny saved is a penny earned" can be applied to some extent here. My second motive is having a gauge to help me prioritize plans on developing the domains on my own – perhaps a simple web site at first displaying Google AdSense ads.

*Interestingly, in my review of various domain parking services, I noticed the ads displayed tend to always be the same. My thought is the services must be utilizing Google's AdSense API for customizing the look and feel of the contextual ads displayed on parked pages.

··· ❹ ···
Designing and Developing your Site

Introduction

You do not need to be a professional designer or web developer to build a successful web site. While it is beneficial to have custom web design and front/back-end programming skill, you generally only need this skill set if you are developing a high-end web application. Content management systems (CMS's) and templates are effective in helping entrepreneurs put together professional quality web sites in little time, with minimal resources (time and money) required. HTML, CSS and basic graphic design/editing skills in Photoshop and Illustrator are handy when you want to make custom modifications to these templates to help make your new site more closely match your brand/idea. If you want to make custom edits to the template, best practice encourages designers and developers to create a sub-theme, which extends functions from the parent theme and only calls items that have been modified. As commercial themes are updated from time to time, this allows one to simply overwrite existing parent theme files without needing to spend the extra time to document changes, compare code in a file comparison program, etc.

Sometimes, technology and know-how aside, one of the most challenging pieces behind web design and development is to decide what your site's focus or niche will be, your audience and what content will go on your site. This should be decided well in advance during a planning phase, before you actually start putting anything together. Otherwise, you may very well end up staring at a blank screen wondering what to do next. You may find it beneficial to start a new Google word processing document to jot down some ideas during a brainstorming session, which you can add to whenever you get more ideas. Once you have an idea, you can start to sketch some ideas on paper and scan to share with others (if you wish with a team or sourced contractors), or there are nice electronic sketch tools such as Pencil (pencil.evolus.vn/en-us/home.aspx) and Balsamiq Mockups (www.balsamiq.com/products/mockups). The latter is widely used in the industry and if by chance you do a lot of volunteer work, you may be eligible for a free personal license.

As you are planning your site or application, do not be afraid to refer to professional designs/themes for inspiration. Another nice book I found a while back, "The Web Design Wow! Book" by Jack Davis and Susan Merritt is a bit dated but still has some nice elements all designers should consider when building their site.

Another important aspect to consider when designing your site or application is you want to entice the user to come back and continue using your product. In other words, it needs to be slick, cutting-edge and look the 'best of the best' with addictive functionality. I have worked in the software industry and can say millions have been invested in hiring top breed User Interface (UI) and User Experience (UX) talent to ensure the design is on par with end-user/customer expectations. An argument can even be made that the design is more important than the code or functionality behind the design as a 'killer look' encourages users to return and look for more features as they get pushed to production.

You should also consider common sense and trends a normal user would expect, such as a site's logo linking back to the home page, not incorporating overly flash graphics (i.e. annoying animated ads with fast refresh rates and cycles, etc.) Also, try to link within your site as much as possible, as that can only strengthen your site's SEO value (described later in this book).

This chapter will not review too many details of web site design and development as it will be beyond the scope of this book, but will review some common practices and share some of the latest trends.

CORE TOOLS

Other web design and development tools will be highlighted elsewhere in this chapter, but some of the more common ones are Adobe's Creative Suite (Web and Print), which includes Dreamweaver, Photoshop, Illustrator, Flash and others. Dreamweaver is a nice WYSIWYG editor and allows people to visually lay out web pages. It also has a built-in FTP editor and subversion/code check-in/out functionality, useful in team environments. Photoshop is great for editing PSD files or creating your own and exporting as transparent PNG files, GIF or JPG files as appropriate. PNG files are popular on the web and are taking the place of GIF files. JPG files are still popular for high-res photos, which tend to get downsized/compressed to at least 80% quality for the web. Illustrator is popular for creating/editing vector graphics and logos, while Flash is still popular for creating animated/interstitial ads and Flash applications. Adobe's product is a commercial suite, but it is cheaper to buy the products as a suite versus a few products individually. They now offer a cloud-based service which is beneficial for slow computers.

GIMP is a nice open source alternative to Photoshop and HTML-Kit is a nice alternative to Dreamweaver if you are on a budget. But to be honest, after 16+ years in the industry and using many free (and paid) alternatives to Adobe's products, I strongly feel the cost/benefit of Adobe's suite far exceeds any other product on the market. Corel's suite would be a close second to Adobe, in my opinion, is much cheaper but does not have all of the same features and lacks the standardization aspect that Adobe's products enjoy. In this case, I believe you get what you pay for.

When you need to upload files to production, a popular FTP program is called FileZilla, available at www.filezilla-project.org. This can also be used to download files if you want to create backups from time to time.

Another core product that becomes useful if you work with CMS products and other web applications is SQLyog. This utility allows you to manage local and remote databases and create database backups. You can download the commercial edition at www.webyog.com, or the community (free) edition at code.google.com/p/sqlyog. Alternatively, phpMyAdmin (www.phpmyadmin.net/home_page) is another nice cloud-based MySQL database management utility that many web hosting providers supply, but this tends to limit the size of a SQL file you can import or export. But a nice utility to make changes on the fly if you do not have SQLyog or similar utility installed on your system.

PIXEL PERFECT DESIGN

Tasked with creating a web page from an Adobe Photoshop (.PSD) file with pixel perfect precision? Here are a few links you may find beneficial, to either introduce you to this topic and/or possibly enhance your skills:

- www.aloestudios.com/2008/08/pixel-precision-with-diagnostic-css
- code.google.com/p/shepherd-interactive/wiki/overlaycomp (tool)
- www.pixelperfectplugin.com (tool)

WEB DESIGN AND DEVELOPMENT TRENDS

Today, responsive/fluid/elastic designs (the terms are interchangeable) are popular and almost critical if you want your site to render properly in multiple devices such as mobile phones, iPads, netbooks, large monitors, etc. Theme frameworks can provide this functionality for you 'out of the box' and you can simply implement your design/design customizations within the theme and benefit from this feature (so long as you do not override this feature). This can save you significant time. However, if you wanted to develop your own theme and media queries (response definitions), you might want to reuse some of the media query definitions available at the "Hardboiled CSS3 Media Queries von Andy Clarke" web site: gist.github.com/1362209. These queries are available through a "Creative Commons CC Zero Declaration" license, which provides good use flexibility.

Also worth noting, many designers and developers tend to design web sites and applications within CSS frameworks. A popular one is called the 960 grid system available at www.960.gs. A modified version of this framework, which includes fluid functionality is called Fluid 960 Grid System which you can download at www.designinfluences.com/fluid960gs. Finally, a "remixed" version of Fluid 960 Grid System is available at www.sanfordsworld.com/fluid960gs-remixed, with some additional functionality. The version you select is really up to your specific needs and preferences. You can also use another popular framework called Foundation (foundation.zurb.com). These frameworks help expedite the process of designing and developing a site, commonly referred to "rapid prototyping." If you build many web sites, this will save you some time recoding your usual CSS classes, essentially a custom framework. By the way, CSS3 is the current standard as of this book and now has good support across browsers, although lacks some support with Internet Explorer. You may need to apply some CSS hacks from time to time, which you can Google.

HTML5 Boilerplate is also a great framework for HTML5 development, available at www.html5boilerplate.com.

jQuery is popular because it is a simplified version of JavaScript ("JS") and is popular with UI Designers and Developers. jQuery UI is popular for developing jQuery UI components, or you can select commercial alternatives such as Kendo UI (www.kendoui.com) which is developed and supported by Telerik, which has a solid reputation. If you would like to compare differences between jQuery UI and Kendo UI, someone built a site dedicated to comparing the two, which you can view at www.jqueryuivskendoui.com. Kendo UI is nice because the developer also provides tools that allow you to easily modify controls through their ThemeBuilder utility (demos.kendoui.com/themebuilder/index.html).

APPLICATION DEVELOPMENT

If your site or application requires some kind of programming aspect and database, PHP and MySQL is commonly used and powers many popular content management systems (CMS) such as Drupal, Joomla and WordPress. These technologies are 'open source', which means you have 100% access to the code and can distribute freely. Java-based applications are also popular, particularly with enterprise software. However, commercial technologies such as ASP.Net are also used to build applications, which involve C# or Visual Basic .Net programming languages.

If you are looking to build a mobile app, you might want to consider taking a look at www.applicationcraft.com for some nice cloud application build options.

TESTING

Manual browser-based testing with Internet Explorer, Firefox, Chrome, Opera and the PC and Mac versions of Safari are suggested, from the most current version to two versions down for each to ensure your site/application renders properly in all browsers. You can automate testing in programs such as Selenium (www.seleniumhq.org), if your site or application changes frequently from a feature and code perspective which can save some time and provide greater 'code coverage' to test as many user paths and possible processes as possible.

CONTENT MANAGEMENT SYSTEMS

CHOOSING A CONTENT MANAGEMENT SYSTEM (CMS)

First, as a caveat (and despite all the hype of CMS's), unless you are a major corporation with thousands of employees requiring the ability to create/maintain web content on-the-fly, the benefits of implementing a static or semi-dynamic web site may outweigh the advantages of a bona-fide Content Management System.

You should ask yourself whether or not you require a site-wide CMS. Publishers for instance may only need a news/article publishing system vs. having the ability to maintain their entire web content collection via the web. Such systems mimic the capability of popular blog systems such as WordPress (www.wordpress.org) and Movable Type (www.movabletype.org) – both very powerful programs.

A downside of using CMS's is the fact that (out of the box) they tend not to rank well within search engines such as Google, Yahoo, MSN, etc. However, there are ways around this using mod_rewrite on UNIX/Linux systems and if you research the web enough, you may find your CMS offers add-ons/enhancements known as modules or plug-ins which can utilize mod_rewrite's ability to automatically parse your web site and create 'search engine friendly' links. This may require a significant amount of time, but depending on your situation practicality of a CMS to you/your organization it may be worth the research.

All of this aside, popular open source CMS systems on the UNIX/Linux end are Drupal (www.drupal.org), Joomla (www.joomla.org) and Mambo (www.mamboserver.com). Drupal is a very advanced system used by Linux Journal, MTV (I believe in England) and many others... the downside of this system is it has a fairly high learning curve. My understanding with Joomla is many of the original core developers from Mambo's team moved on to create Joomla so it mimics many of the basic capabilities of Mambo and is now slightly more advanced. Mambo is not a bad CMS however, was developed before Joomla and has a large community base you can use for support and is still being improved upon to date by qualified software engineers.

On the Windows end, you may want to consider looking at either DotNetNuke (www.dotnetnuke.com) or one of Ektron's CMS's (www.ektron.com). DotNetNuke is open source software and has a very large support base although support is limited to a forum where inquiries and responses must first be approved by a moderator which can delay response time. Ektron offers their CMS's at-cost but they offer solid CMS products used by companies such as Yahoo, BAE Systems, etc. and you can talk to a real person when you need to by picking up the phone. Ektron offers CMS400.Net (based on ASP.Net) and CMS300 (having slightly less features and based on classic ASP)... you can review the various features via www.ektron.com/cms400-web-cms.aspx?id=1757.

Taking into consideration everyone's content management needs differ, you may want to take a look at even more options available for review at www.opensourcecms.com that may more specifically match the solution you are looking for. This site lists all the major CMS's and allows you to test-drive the front-end and administrative back-end on-demand (through their web site) vs. needing to first install on your web server and then evaluate. Google, as you may know is a great search engine for finding even more CMS options if you want to consider a commercial product instead.

And if you decide a CMS is not right for you, search engine results suggest a static/semi-static web site ranks higher than CMS-driven web sites so you have a positive here. Your organization can also manage your web site using a product called Adobe Contribute CS3 (formerly Macromedia Contribute) which allows you to assign users a key allowing them to manage certain areas of your web site while limiting their administrative permissions in the process (i.e. whether or not they can delete files, etc.)

WORDPRESS - NOT JUST A BLOG PLATFORM

WordPress (www.wordpress.com), a popular open-source blogging platform written in PHP/MySQL has a plethora of built-in search engine optimization features built-in, making the software desirable to independent web entrepreneurs and established businesses alike.

I particularly like WordPress's built-in SEO system utilizing Apache's mod_rewrite capabilities (URL rewriting). I've evaluated various open source CMS products and noticed (based on my experience alone, working on very targeted, niche-centric sites) that search engines such as Google tend to favor content delivered WordPress over other platforms such as Joomla. To clarify, I am speaking of the CMS's default, build-in SEO features. There are certainly many plug-ins - both free/open source and commercial - you can install for popular CMS products such as Joomla that are designed to enhance the default SEO functionality.

Previously, I stayed away from utilizing WordPress for many of my web sites due to the obvious blog-style architecture (I was looking for a bona-fide CMS appearance). However, there are a number of commercial WordPress templates available to you for low cost (and even some decent free templates) that are designed to leverage WordPress's core CMS capabilities by delivering content such as articles in a more traditional CMS style. A popular commercial WordPress template developer is WooThemes – www.woothemes.com – you can purchase a subscription to access various templates or you can purchase templates on an individual basis as well. If your budget is limited, you will sacrifice some of the nice features made available with these commercial templates but if you 'don't need a Porche' as they say, there are a number of very nice open-source templates available for download at the WordPress template depository - www.wordpress.org/extend/themes.

I've heard a few professionals indicate using WordPress beyond a blogging platform, as a true CMS product can experience some growing pains if you wish to upgrade the core system, add more features via installation of 3rd party plug-ins, etc. Performance may not be optimum as well, per the system being designed for blogging. But the advantages may outweigh the disadvantages per WordPress's solid SEO capabilities and ease of use.

A top SEO strategist and forerunner in emerging web marketing research reported at a Washington, DC Specialized Information Publishing Association (SIPA) conference in June 2007 that they like to utilize this platform specifically for its excellent SEO capabilities. So there is definitely additional some proof out there to validate the use of WordPress as a true CMS platform vs. merely for blogging.

AUTOMATIC CONTENT GENERATION

A sub-set of Internet marketing involves automatic content generation. A quick review of some of the tools available in this area suggests the content is generated from RSS feeds you program into the tool's back-end/configuration area. (Disclaimer: I suggest you read into these tools a bit more as I have not personally used any of these programs as of yet.)

A few of these programs you may be interested in:

- WordPress AutoBlogged - www.autoblogged.com (did not respond to an e-mail inquiry of mine regarding links to sample sites created with this tool but still might be legitimate – saw them advertised on Facebook ads)
- WP AutoBlogger - www.wpautoblogger.com

- AutoBlogger Pro - www.autobloggerpro.com

The tools are a bit pricey but they may prove to be an excellent investment if leveraged appropriately. But before opening your wallet, you may want to take a look at an open source alternative – which I consider an excellent CMS designed for a niche group involved with online news publication. This program is called Pligg (www.pligg.com) and appears to have a solid community base supporting further development of the software. If this program does not have all the features available with the commercial applications, you should have no problem finding a freelance PHP/MySQL programmer on the web that can implement those features for you.

On the subject of blogging, you might be interested in visiting www.problogger.net for useful tips and resources geared to help you become a successful blogger. The author of this site apparently is able to make a living blogging full time so you should be able to learn quite a bit here.

RSS is a Valuable Tool that Helps you Maximize your Marketing Campaign's Reach

Web marketers who stride with the idea that SEO is limited primarily to META tags, site architecture (i.e. properly formatted path names and file names in URLs), and writing SEO-friendly content (typically involving clever embedding of relational keywords/phrases within context) are misled. This is only half of the battle – getting your site's pages linked elsewhere is also a critical component towards a successful SEO strategy.

To get started, FeedBurner (www.feedburner.com) is an excellent tool that allows web marketers to easily track how many people are subscribed to their RSS feed(s) while offering a historical analysis of your feed's popularity and a breakdown of your feed's most popular content (such as the top 5 headlines your visitors clicked on, etc.) What you want to do is create a Feedburner account if you don't already have one and burn feed links through their web site that link to your feed's XML file stored on your server.

Your next step is to publicize the feeds (click on the "Publicize" tab in FeedBurner). The following are 2 excellent tools you can use to publicize your RSS feeds:

BuzzBoost - This is an excellent tool that allows web designers/developers of varying skill levels to easily display your feed's content on their web site (i.e. top 10 headlines from your feed with a brief description). This works great with search engines and benefits those who syndicate your content on their web sites by populating their pages with relevant content that appeals to their audience.

PingShot - This will automatically list your feeds with services such as Technorati, Newsgator, Ping-o-matic, Feed Crier, Alexa and many others.

A word of caution: beware of 'link bombs' - such as when a blogger has an unusually high amount of friends link to his or her blog in a short period of time. Google and other search engines pick up on this and can quickly classify your site as spam. Best advice is to allow people to gradually introduce displaying your feeds on their site while participating in a link exchange program... generally a good idea - whereas you setup a formal link directory page or section on your web site and encourage those you link to to link back to your site as a favor. For more info on this, Google "reciprocal link exchange programs".

··· ❺ ···
E-COMMERCE

A few well-known e-commerce companies would be eBay and Amazon.com. These are multi-million dollar companies that have remained successful ever since the Internet has become popular, largely because of their investments in optimizing online order fulfillment and processing and emphasis on user interface design and experience. These investments have likely amounted to millions of dollars.

Entrepreneurs have been successful copying strategies implemented by companies such as eBay and Amazon.com, particularly in niche areas and/or in other geographies. It is relatively easy to sell your own products through an online shopping cart, or dropship third party products. Similarly, many have become successful by simply serving as an affiliate – either by featuring select products or via a virtual storefront integrated with various affiliate programs/vendors.

E-COMMERCE STRATEGIES

Top strategies that may contributes towards increased web revenue include:

- **Listing your items on product comparison web sites** and carefully monitoring success via click-throughs, etc. and optimizing the feeds as necessary.
- **Listing your items for sale on eBay**, via an eBay storefront.
- **Creating two storefronts**, each acting as if they are separate with varying SEO/marketing strategy tactics used (this helps to determine what the best e-commerce strategy to use is).
- **Applying to be a supplier** with Internet-based wholesalers such as Doba.com and Shopster.com.

- **Sell your products on Amazon.com** (create a merchant account).
- In terms of getting your products to brick and mortar retail stores, you may want to **consider supplying to traditional wholesalers** (not Internet based) and start negotiation channels with those responsible for purchasing new items (i.e. I believe Wal-Mart does all their purchasing and selection from their home office).
- This one would take some time to develop but may be worth the investment... you can **offer customer support, order fulfillment/distribution, returns, etc. to entrepreneurs** who want to sell your products by creating portals displaying your products they can arrange and mark up under the vise of their own store logo/branding, etc. 'in partnership' with company X (if you don't want to use your current company name as the trademark).

STREAMLINE PAYMENT OPTIONS - MAKE IT EASY FOR CUSTOMERS TO BUY WHAT THEY WANT!

If you offer products/services for sale on your site, be sure to offer multiple payment options for your customers. Sometimes, easily overlooked pieces such as this can be cause for a potential customer to move on, especially for certain age groups (i.e. younger audience that may not have a credit card), or certain regions in the world. I digress slightly, but on the subject I recommend at least offering credit card acceptance through PayPal, Google Checkout, Authorize.net or 2CheckOut as these are among the most popular. A way to accept direct deposit/bank transfer from a bank account, personal check usage (e-check), cash and money orders is also helpful. You should use caution accepting money orders however as many scammers use this form of payment and the person accepting the money order does not realize it was counterfeit until after they sent a product. A security scan service is also beneficial as it regularly scans/protect your site from hackers and gives your customers confidence that their transactions and visits are secure. Some of the more popular services in this area include TRUSTe, McAfee Secure, VeriSign Secured, Trustwave Trusted Commerce, MasterCard SecureCode and Verified by VISA. If applicable, it also helps to include a logo that shows you are a BBB Accredited Business, BizRate award, Fortune 500, 1000 status, etc. These tend to be placed in the site's footer (which, as an aside, should never come across as a design oversight).

SEARCH ENGINE OPTIMIZATION AND MARKETING (SEO/SEM)

SEO is valuable as it serves as a control mechanism for helping publishers keep their content relevant, original and presenting information on web pages that load quickly, benefiting the end-user and ultimately the publisher/retailer. Organic SEO (as opposed to paid search marketing, such as what you see on the top, right and bottom side of Google.com search engines) is a 'free'/low-cost method of increasing your web page/site rankings to appear in the top ten search results, preferably in the top five as it is 'above the fold'. Most people do not browse beyond the top ten search results/first page and try another search query.

Copywriting is a large focus area in search engine optimization. Many SEO professionals subscribe to the idea that content (quality, depth, relevancy, uniqueness) is the #1 element that works towards a site's successful ranking. In fact, many SEO professionals use the phrase "content is king." Generally, the more relevant and unique content that can be added to these sites, the better for SEO/rankings.

Some people like to generate SEO by pulling in external content, from off-site RSS feeds for instance. This is not optimal because you will not gain SEO value for the content displayed on your site because it originated elsewhere, and the links tied to the RSS articles will take a user to another site. This means you will not benefit from pageviews, but the links can help define your site in a certain niche by your users and search engines if mixed in with other content. RSS feeds providing the bulk of the content for a web site are common with portal sites – Alltop (www.alltop.com) for instance.

It is important to recognize that optimizing an element on a web site, e-newsletter and other media is not necessarily attributed to improving SEO, especially if a resource is not visible to search engines. I have heard at least one person incorrectly refer to online media improvements as SEO, but it is important to remember SEO strictly relates to optimizing a page or site's content to achieve improved rankings in popular search engines. SEO is a subset of Internet marketing and not all marketing improvements have perceived effects on how well a page ranks.

With Google Universal Search, you no longer just get text-based search results. At times, you can get results from other Google databases (images, Google News, videos from YouTube, results from Google Local, books and other products from Google Base, etc.) so it is always good to source data to these databases as well, where applicable. For instance, a news publisher might want to apply for submission to Google News if they have not done so already because it can help boost traffic to their web site(s)... many simply log right into the Google News site. Google Images is a good place to get listed as well because clicking on a thumbnail takes the user to your web site.

YouTube is the world's third largest search engine, and it is valuable to get listed on this site for the additional exposure. You can create 'how to' videos and other video formats to get found directly in YouTube and also have videos shown in Google's search results from time to time, as they relate to search queries.

IF YOU SEEK AN SEO CONSULTANT...

Despite what some SEO professionals may tell you, there is no surefire method to increase organic (free) search engine results in Google, Yahoo, Bing or any other popular search engine. If an SEO professional guarantees or otherwise has some kind of warranty to back their work up, you should ask by what date results are guaranteed by, and more importantly, how long those results are warranted to stay in place for. The latter is important to consider because someone can easily perform what is known as a 'Google Bomb' where they place comment spam with links to push more traffic and increase page one rankings, but since these non-ethical practices can blacklist your site and would otherwise be somewhat temporary (due to Google's advanced legitimacy algorithms, etc.), you should carefully review and select a quality SEO professional and ask for trusted references you can call.

No SEO 'Secret Recipe' Exists

When applying SEO concepts, it is important to keep in mind that there is no secret recipe for improving results. Common practices exist, which will be outlined in this chapter that every good designer, developer and marketer should follow and use as a quasi-checklist when creating or modifying their web sites. Furthermore, in order to rank above your competition and get the results you are looking for, SEO should never be considered an after-thought and should be more of an integrated approach. If you follow and implement SEO best practices and regularly research the latest SEO/SEM trends via Google's blog and other SEO blogs with articles written by the industry's top performers, you will have an edge over those that only do just enough to get by.

It is important to not apply too much focus on SEO and keep in mind that SEO is only one piece of your overall marketing strategy. If you design and develop your site correctly and post quality, relevant content for your audience, good rankings tend to happen naturally. Too much SEO focus can actually hurt your rankings because search engines view this as 'black hat marketing'. You should always keep your visitor in mind and never design/develop your site exclusively with SEO in mind – there needs to be a good balance between the two, with preference given to your user base.

SEO REPORTING TOOLS

I heard good things about a program called SEOmoz (www.seomoz.org) to make SEO reviews/analysis easier for in-house staff to manage which gives some helpful advice on what to do to increase rankings. WebCEO (www.webceo.com) is also a good tool I used before that does the same thing. The tools can be configured to run on a semi-automatic or automatic/scheduled basis to get up-to-date reports on your site's rankings.

Many SEO Consultants use SEOmoz for preliminary research to see how well a site ranks (among other criteria) and then expands on the generated report(s) with their own real-world experience and knowledge of SEO trends from courses, industry blogs, events/trade shows, user groups, peer to peer knowledge sharing and other sources. If you have the budget to hire an SEO Consultant, I highly recommend doing so to get the most complete picture of what is working and identifying areas of improvement. However, these programs are also a good budget solution to start with and perhaps hand off to a consultant later on if you wanted to further improve rankings, get clarification on items from the report, etc.

A few other tools:

- Google Analytics - great 3rd party tool to identify demographics, visits, pageviews, time spent on site, keywords/phrases used to find your site, list of sites that referred a visitor to your site, etc.
- Self-hosted web analytics alternative - piwiki
- Paid alternatives – WebTrends and Coremetrics
- Google Keyword Suggestion tool (free) - Gold standard for keyword/phrase discovery as it identifies/suggests which keywords and associated keywords you may want to use on

your site (integrating in your site's copy, link/path structure, hyperlinking, etc.) A few related search tools:

- o Google Trends - www.google.com/trends
- o Google Trends (Hot Searches) - www.google.com/trends/hottrends
- o Google Insights for Search - www.google.com/insights/search
- Paid keyword suggestion alternatives, mixed with some free ones:
  - o Trellian Keyword Discovery – www.keyworddiscovery.com/search.html
  - o Keyword Research - www.ispionage.com
  - o YouTube Promoted Videos - ads.youtube.com/keyword_tool
  - o Wordtracker - freekeywords.wordtracker.com
  - o Wordstream - www.wordstream.com/keywords
  - o Google Reader (to spot trends) - www.google.com/reader/view
  - o Compete – www.compete.com/us
  - o Microsoft Advertising Intelligence - advertising.microsoft.com/small-business/adcenter-downloads/microsoft-advertising-intelligence
  - o Trendistic (Twitter search trends) - trendistic.indextank.com
  - o Twitter search - twitter.com/#!/search-home
  - o Wordtracker Google Trends - freekeywords.wordtracker.com/gtrends
  - o SEO Report Tools - www.urltrends.com
  - o eBay Pulse - pulse.ebay.com
- CSS image sprite creator (to reduce image load time) - www.spriteme.org
- Adobe Photoshop (image optimization)

- Firefox plugin called Page Speed – requires Firebug (dependency), another Firefox add-on. "Page speed test" or "Fully Loaded" are good equivalents for Chrome.
- Google Webmaster - view your site in the eyes of search engines/Google specifically
- CSS Compressor & Minifier - www.minifycss.com/css-compressor
- Firefox/Chrome plug-in called WebRank Toolbar - the toolbar can instantly tell you how a site ranks as you visit them.

Search engine/directory/URL submission tools and services influence your rankings less today but are still important. Of these tools, the most popular may be Trellian SubmitWolf v8.0, which marketers use to automate URL submission to search engines: www.trellian.com/swolf

Note: to be best assured your site did in fact get submitted, you may want to consider manually submitting your site to at least the top search engines and automated submission to 2nd, 3rd tier/rate search engines.

RANKING METRICS

A nice Firefox/Chrome plug-in called WebRank Toolbar can instantly tell you how a site ranks as you visit them. This is a nice tool you can use to determine some SEO metrics. Some popular metrics you should take note of are noted below:

- Google PageRank
- Alexa Rank
- Pages indexed in Google, Bing and Yahoo
- Backlinks according to Google, Bing and Yahoo

GOOGLE NEWS

To see if your web site is indexed in Google News, go to www.google.com/news and query site:X, where X is the domain name (i.e. site:yourdomain.com).

If your site is not currently indexed with Google News, you can put in a request to have your publication reviewed and indexed. Sometimes this process might take a day or so, other times weeks as the application generally involves a manual review. If you do not hear anything on your application after say two weeks, do not be afraid to gently follow-up with Google to see if they have any new information regarding your index status.

Initially, after a new index, you may see traffic will spike in a few hours after you get indexed, which may last a day or so. This is especially true if you had all historical and current articles referenced in a separate Google News XML feed, rendering all or most of the articles getting indexed/discoverable in Google News.

It may help to have article ID numbers included at the end of URLs you submit to Google News, although this is not a requirement if you use XML sitemaps for the news feeds. If you do include article numbers in your URLs, you might want to consider creating subdirectories beyond your "news" directory (i.e. news/features/article-789). The latter helps the ID go beyond 999.

You may want to review the following Google support links for some more information on these concepts:

- www.google.com/support/news_pub/bin/answer.py?hl=en&answer=68323
- www.google.com/support/news_pub/bin/answer.py?answer=74288

SITE MAP

Site maps are important because they help guide search engines as they index your web site. You can reference some or all of your site's web pages and, optionally, set priority levels for each one, while suggesting the frequency of search engine spiders to revisit your site.

SEO best practices call for web site administrators to create a static (traditional) HTML site map that is linked from the site's footer, in addition to creating a regular XML site map and a news XML site map (if the latter applies). Setting these site maps up helps boost SEO because search engines have access to all files and can quickly scan a site map, potentially revisiting/indexing pages faster.

As true for other many other aspects of SEO, one needs to be careful not to abuse XML file priority or revisit settings or this might impact the index values Google and other search engines assign to your web pages. For example, in most cases, you do not want to set all of your pages to have a 1.0 priority level with an hourly revisit. Potential red flags aside, most search engines do not have the bandwidth to revisit entire web sites at this frequency.

Here are a few recommended values:

- Home page: 1.0 priority with a daily revisit setting
- Section index pages (i.e. About Us): 0.6-0.9 with a daily revisit setting. If it is a news index page, you can change the revisit frequency to hourly.
- Regular pages: 0.5 priority level with a weekly revisit setting

Some publishers may be inclined to have all of their web page files in a single XML site map file. This practice is not encouraged because it places a burden on search engine bots/spiders, especially if this file exceeds 500 or more links. As a result, many break this file down into smaller chunks that are linked from the master XML site map file. Many content management systems such as WordPress or Drupal, to name a few can be set up to handle this task automatically through third party plugins/modules.

PATHS IN URLS

Some people may not realize this, but the way your web site's URL is configured plays an important role in how well your pages get indexed.

If you are creating a new site, or might be open to moving your existing site to a new domain, you might want to register (or buy an existing domain from someone) that is short, easy to remember and has various keywords/phrases included in the domain. Domains with the .com suffix tend to rank best over other top-level domains (TLDs).

Pages that are setup in the following format: www.yourdomain.com/page-with-keywords.html tend to perform well over page names that are further away from the base domain. Along the same idea, if you consider breadcrumb structure, where the parent category is usually listed first, followed by a sub-category and so on, the same concept should apply to URL structure for the best rankings. Using dashes for spaces is recommended over underscores ("_") or %20 (the HTML equivalent for spaces). I also recommend organizing your structure similar to the breadcrumb concept, for instance: www.yourdomains.com/news/todays-news/article-title.html

If your site has a news section, I highly recommend creating a "news" directory attached to your domain. This allows search engines to recognize this content as news and they may be inclined to revisit/index this area more frequently. An important aspect if you want your content to appear in Google News and other news sources.

If you use Google's Keyword Suggestion tool, you can find some nice keywords/phrases to use for your directory and page names.

META Information in Page Header Source

Another valuable SEO strategy is to place META keyword and description code in your site's home page and inside-site page source.

The keywords and descriptions should preferably vary and not be the same throughout the web site. At the very least, you should create a set of keywords and a description for the home page, section pages and actual content pages (i.e. article, product, etc.) I also suggest the keywords and descriptions used reflect some of the related keywords found for specific keywords/phrases from the Google Keyword Suggestion tool.

Page descriptions should not be treated as an oversight or 'quick fix'. For instance, a short description for a travel site that uses "Plan your visit to Bar Harbor Maine" works but you could gain higher SEO value by having some more subject-matter keywords in the description.

META keywords and descriptions are no longer valued as much as they used to be, at least in the eyes of today's search engines. That was not the case many years ago but one aspect that changed this was competitors would copy META tag data from top performing pages/sites and reuse these on their sites to realize similar rankings. With this said however, META keywords and descriptions are still important because it helps search engines categorize pages.

Beyond META keyword and description tags, it is also a good idea to configure another tag that dictates to what extent Google and other search engines should visit your site:
<meta name="robots" content="index, follow">

When you configure page META data, you will want to use competitive keywords/phrases sparingly. If you go overboard, your site could be flagged as spam, which would impact your site's ranking.

When you put together SEO ranking reports, you may want to consider copying the list of top 100-250 keywords/phrases from Google Analytics' report for the last 30 days. You can then paste this list in an SEO analysis program, which will tell you how well these keywords/phrases rank with various search engines. This should provide you with a fairly accurate idea of how well these keywords and phrases are performing and you can adjust the META keywords and descriptions accordingly. As an aside, if you find certain target keywords/phrases are not performing well, you can try writing more content on your site to help your pages get found for those queries.

PAGE LOAD TIME TESTING

A Firefox plugin called Page Speed is an excellent tool you can use to determine how quickly your pages load and then make improvements accordingly. Page Speed requires Firebug, another Firefox plugin to operate.

Why is it important to review how quickly your pages load? Search engines have limited bandwidth as they scan and index new and existing pages on your site. As a result, the faster a page loads, the more pages a search engine can scan during a single session. Recall that web sites typically contain dozens, if not hundreds or thousands of web pages and these cannot all get scanned at once, even if you incorporate XML sitemaps. Beyond the index component, Google and other search engines review how quickly your pages load to place a quality value with your site. Naturally, they try to avoid listing slow-loading web sites in top ten organic search results.

Here are a few ways a web administrator can improve a web page's load time:

- External CSS and JavaScript files should be combined into as few files as possible. Many times, if a site uses a CMS, there may be various CSS and JS files referenced in a page's HEAD area that should be consolidated, where possible.
- Minify CSS and JavaScript code. This means removing extra spaces within the code, unnecessary/duplicate CSS, etc.
- Images should always include height and width attributes, either within the HTML or the class/ID associated with the image.
- CSS sprites can drastically improve the time it takes your browser to download images. www.spriteme.org is a good service that can help you with this task if you do not have access to Photoshop.
- Public-facing images should be optimized whenever possible. Typically, I optimize JPG, GIF and PNG images to 80% quality within Photoshop and occasionally further – so long as it does not visibly impact the overall quality of the graphic.

If your development software or CMS allows you to do this, you can be creative and help increase page load times by having the public-facing code generated by your pages appear on one line, with all spaces, line returns, etc. removed. You can also use caching and throttling techniques.

LINK BUILDING STRATEGIES

PR SEO

Press release (PR) submission engines can greatly enhance the amount of backlinks (links on external web sites that point back to your site).

One popular PR submission site that has some free PR submission options is PitchEngine (www.pitchengine.com).

If you had a budget set aside for paid PR submission, I highly recommend PRWeb (www.prweb.com). I say this because I have seen PR content rank very well after getting indexed here, perhaps because Google recognizes you are spending money with this service, as opposed to using free PR submission channels that are sometimes abused by spammers. PR Newswire (www.prnewswire.com) is another great paid alternative.

Basically, the idea behind PR SEO is that when you send a press release to PR engines, your submission will get noticed by others in your industry and they will copy the PR to their site or summarize your PR for inclusion on their site with links pointing back to your site. The more people that do this, the more backlinks created which further defines your Internet presence.

OTHER LINK BUILDING STRATEGIES

Here are a few other strategies you might want to consider as you focus on creating more backlinks for your site:

- Does your site have a blog? If not, you might want to consider having one for the SEO benefit. Then, you can link target keywords/phases to associated pages on your site.
- Ask the owner of a popular web site/blog if you can submit a free blog post that compliments the site's subject matter. If they are OK with this, see if you can provide one or more links within your post that refer back to your site.
- Provided the owner of a blog is OK with this, you can get additional traffic to your site by providing a link back to your site within blog/page comments, or within your signature that may appear in each comment. Be careful with this however as

you do not want your comments to be considered comment spam – you want it to be relevant to the content and make it appear seamless to the reader as an integrated reply to an article.

- Twitter is an excellent platform to micro-blog about almost any topic, which for some sites is the number one traffic source. Just remember to keep your audience in mind and keep all posts relevant. 'How to' posts are popular, in addition to sharing links to new products/services, videos, reviews and more.

- Link/banner exchange programs are also valuable. These used to be more commonplace, but should never be overlooked, especially if you can work out an agreement to get your link(s) placed on high PageRank sites.

(Cockrum, 2011, pp. 62-63)

GETTING LISTED ON PARTNER SITES / INDUSTRY EXPERT BLOG SITES

In the Link Building Strategies section, I shared a few ways you can build backlinks. The best backlinks are the ones incorporated on relevant partner sites and industry thought leader sites so I wanted to focus on this area a bit more.

If you go to a site called SimilarSites.com (www.similarsites.com), you can get a list of web sites that may pertain to your niche. From here, you can find the site owner's contact information via a WHOIS query (you can go to domaintools.com or use GoDaddy's WHOIS tool to find this) and then try to work out a deal to get listed on their site. You will of course want to make sure the sites rank in the top 10 results in Google, Yahoo and Bing for this to be worthwhile (against your target keywords and phrases). The sites should also have a good PageRank, perhaps anything 5 or above. A Firefox plugin called WebRank

Toolbar works great to help you determine how well a site ranks as you review them.

One important item to note is if you work out a link swap, where you agree to place another's link on your site and they do the same for your site's URL, that the links are not randomly placed somewhere on the site. If a page is link heavy, Google might consider this a devious attempt to circumvent its algorithm to increase your site's traffic. In other words, the location of the link is important to get the most out of the arrangement – both for yourself and those viewing the page will be more inclined to click on it, especially if it has a link name and brief description of your site.

Some publishers like to trade RSS feed links, which get converted to HTML. These feeds typically produce regularly-updated news that sends traffic to the source site. While the latter may not be the best case scenario for the party hosting the RSS feed, beyond providing a service for their visitors (because it sends traffic away and the host site does not get credit from search engine spiders/bots as they are external URL's), it does create more backlinks which can be a win-win for both parties involved with the trade. The key is that the feeds are converted to HTML, versus dynamically generated JavaScript. You might want to consider including a brief blurb beneath the generated feed links to brand your content (i.e. a "sponsored by" notation or something similar).

Link trade programs can work very well but you will still want to visit the partner sites every so often to confirm your links are still functioning properly. Similarly, you should test the links placed on your site, provided by the partner company to ensure they are not getting redirected to unapproved sources. Determining whether the links are still live is important as well because broken links can impact how well your site ranks in organic search results.

Beyond getting listed on industry niche sites, I also recommend submitting your site to directories and sites that otherwise provide links associated with specific subject matter:

- Open Directory Project (ODP)
- LookSmart
- Yahoo! Directory
- Wikipedia
- Various directories you may find on the Internet that focus on your niche

SUBMITTING CONTENT TO SOCIAL MEDIA AND NEWS AGGREGATION SITES

Many people understand the concept of viral marketing. The more times a reader shares your content on Twitter, Digg, StumbleUpon, Delicious and other sources, the more traffic your site will receive. You should create traditional HTML-based content you publish on your site(s), in addition to posting content on social media sites. For this reason, if you do not already have one account with each of the popular social media channels, you should consider creating one. Beyond the viral marketing benefit, your content posted on social media sites could also very well get indexed by Google and other search engines.

Google+ and Facebook allow you to create pages that users can follow to build a good follow base and additional traffic sourced from each of these social media sites and indexed content. Facebook allows you to create a custom URL for your pages after 25 people "like" the page (in the format facebook.com/X, where X is your custom alias). You can configure this alias by going to www.facebook.com/username . You should keep in mind that you can only configure a vanity alias once and cannot change it unless Facebook changes it for you from their side. So you will want to make sure you are happy with what you enter, from a branding and SEO standpoint – also making sure there are no typos.

LinkedIn can also be a great source for indexed content that can point back to your web site. With LinkedIn, you can do this through what are called "groups" – open or closed areas where you or others can invite people to join to collaborate and share ideas. If the group is open, anyone can join at-will, but if it is closed, they would need an invitation. The important piece to keep in mind with LinkedIn groups is that only open groups will get indexed in search engines, due to the nature of closed groups where none of the content is publically accessible.

Many times, marketers may only pursue the usual social media channels but overlook YouTube and others. YouTube is among the world's most popular search engines so you can get some additional branding and SEO value out of this site, in addition to others you may use. You can promote events, 'how to' videos, full-scale training programs, products and services, even high-value properties if you are in the Real Estate business. Beyond the traffic from YouTube, its videos are commonly indexed by Google because Google owns YouTube and tries to cross-promote material hosted there. Not all videos get indexed in Google, but if you do some research and optimize the title and description of your videos accordingly, you can increase the odds of getting placed within top ten Google organic search results.

Here are a few other sources you might be interested in submitting your content to:

Blog search engines:

- Ask.com(www.ask.com)
- Bloglines (www.bloglines.com)
- Google Blog Search (blogsearch.google.com)

- Technorati (www.technorati.com)

RSS search engines/promotion sites (you would submit your RSS feed links):

- FeedBurner (www.feedburner.com)
- Plazoo (www.plazoo.com)

As you post new content on your web site, consider incorporating scripts (either available from the social media sites, likely somewhere within your account dashboard, or as third party plugins/modules) that automatically add the number of times your article/page was shared. For instance, if it was shared on Twitter, it would feature the number of "Tweets", or if it was shared on LinkedIn, it would show the number of times it was shared. Similarly, you can publicize the number of times content was shared or liked by Facebook users. These features encourage community participation on your site, while helping you promote your content.

As you enhance integration of social media on your site, do not forget to promote your accounts/pages by placing icons in your site's header and/or footer. Some users might like to follow your social media accounts or read historical posts, so this is a great way to guide them to this information.

TRANSLATING CONTENT TO MULTIPLE LANGUAGES

Translating your content to other languages might be cause for some hesitation due to time/resource limitations, not to mention a potential skills gap to handle this task, unless you outsource the translations. I have worked with companies that have selectively converted their content to one or two alternative languages that are popular with their audience. For example, translating English content to Spanish and French. They might not convert all of their content as well, perhaps just their core marketing material to begin with, and perhaps an occasional news/PR piece.

Content translations introduce new content to your site and also enable those who may not speak your language to read your site's material. This increases the number of pages that get indexed by search engines, as well as enhancing traffic to your site, particularly if a user manually configures a certain language of content their search engine should retrieve (if their region-specific search engine does not already do this for them).

Search engines are increasingly placing a higher value on credibility ratings on web sites and, in my opinion, search engines will place a higher ranking for sites that manually convert their content to other languages. Automatic conversions are not entirely accurate, or if they come close, the dialect may be too formal and so on. But if you need to start with automatic translations, that is OK as long as you are confident the content is getting properly translated with at least a 95% accuracy. Remember, you do not want to focus on getting higher traffic – you also want to ensure those reading the content will be able to seamlessly read your material and it is intriguing enough for them to return in the future.

GOOGLE PLACES / DIRECTORY SUBMISSION SITES

I highly recommend all businesses that have at least one physical location to get listed on Google Places. This is because Google Places listings can get placed within top ten search results in Google. Once you complete your listing, you can potentially get indexed within a few days. It is fairly easy to adjust your listing to achieve a desirable index value as well.

As you create your Google Places listing, keep in mind there is currently a 200 character restriction for descriptions. The description and any other data you provide, such as categories, should factor in the keyword/phrase optimizations described earlier in this SEO/SEM chapter (i.e. use Google's Keyword Suggestion tool). Just be careful not to overuse competitive keywords and phrases. The more information and content you provide with your listing (such as images), the more it will stand out in Google's organic search results if you get listed there – or in Google+ Local or Google Maps.

While Google Places might be the most popular directory submission service, do not overlook others. Manta (www.manta.com) is another popular business directory that gets indexed well. If your company promotes events or trade shows, a few other directories you may want to consider are:

- BizTradeShows.com (www.biztradeshows.com)
- Eventful (www.eventful.com)
- TSNN (www.tsnn.com)

SATELLITE SITES

Satellite sites, also referred to as product (or service) specific web sites, can help boost SEO for your brand. Internet marketers tend to register a .com domain name with target keywords/phrases included in the domain. A .com tends to have higher SEO value over .net and others. You should register the domain for at least 2 years and more if you can as spammers tend to register domains for a short while and this will help lead search engines view your site better.

You have to be careful when creating satellite sites because these can easily be flagged as a site trying to 'beat' Google's algorithm. You should never have these on the same IP address as your main web site because your IP address can get flagged as well.

With these sites, it is important to be as honest as possible – you can create optimized copy, include various relevant images, etc. but you should not go overboard. Within a few weeks to two months, you should start to see your site ranked well, provided your keywords and phrases are not overly competitive.

Remember, don't over-use competitive keywords/phrases in context in web sites or the page/site could be flagged as a spam site, or lose Google PageRank points.

THE COMPETITION

A competitive analysis is another critical element of your SEO/SEM strategy. After all, you want to beat your competition, so you want to identify all of your competitors, even a few which might be 'under the radar'. You will also want to understand what your competition is doing to achieve top organic search results so you can make appropriate adjustments.

A good starting point might be to go to www.similarsites.com and enter your web site's URL (or a known competitor you frequently see show up in search results, if you have not yet launched your web site). While SimilarSites.com may not produce completely accurate results, it can provide you with a fairly good picture of associated web sites you may want to consider with your competitive analysis. Of course, you will also want to enter a few manual queries in Google to gather some additional sites to create a comprehensive listing.

Once you build a good list of competitor sites, your next step is to manually review each one and take notes on similarities you see on all of the top-ranked sites. This exercise also gives you an opportunity to make a list of items you like and perhaps ones you do not like so much from a design/feature standpoint that might help you improve your existing site or design a new one. But, you should focus on elements you believe cause the site to rank higher than others, particularly for competitive keywords. You should look at the public-facing layer, in addition to reviewing the code behind the page. In many cases, top-ranking sites will have many cross-links from various areas on the page (i.e. sidebar, header, footer, within the page, etc.) and feature an intelligent architecture and easy-to-navigate interface. The site may have a nice keyword-centric domain name with a properly formatted URL structure and have a nice amount of optimized, original content. These sites tend to have new content introduced fairly regularly and a fair amount of backlinks to support its position in organic search results.

OTHER INFORMATION

It is good to cross-link throughout the site, where appropriate. Many times, a site will have some links setup in the site footer which is very good. If there are any other important content areas you'd like to be consistently reviewed (and hopefully re-indexed often) by search engines, this is a good area to include them. A clever way of cross-linking which also helps to increase pageviews is to link keywords/phrases in articles to other sections of the site.

When you use Google's Keyword Suggestion tool to find keywords and/or related keywords, don't focus on marketing with the top keywords unless you already have a solid rank position for those words/phrases. Instead, I recommend focusing towards the top 80-90% region of the list as anything listed closer to the top of the list generally reflects the most popular (and thus more competitive) keywords. It is sometimes more efficient to get ranked on other words that are still relevant to your subject matter, while still providing for a worthwhile traffic boost.

A good SEM/PPC tip – many people tend to avoid PPC campaigns (i.e. Google AdWords) because it can be very costly. However, if you are careful to set daily budget limits and pause campaigns when necessary and don't focus on competitive keywords, it should not be too costly and could translate to a good investment. A lesser-known strategy involves targeting specific web sites to display your ads on to help reduce the cost. If you do the latter, I'd recommend doing some research to determine which sites 1) rank high in Google and 2) of these sites, which of them display Google AdSense ads on them. Some SEO experts argue that if Google sees you spend some money with an AdWords campaign (or paid PR campaign such as with PR Web for instance), that further differentiates you from other sites making a site appear (again, in Google's eyes) as more credible, thus opening the door for higher rankings.

Regarding image ALT tags, it is good SEO practice to have ALT tags configured for all images. The ALT tags (and the image file names) should reflect subject-matter keywords, where appropriate (not to be abused).

Link TITLE tags are good SEO practice too – example implementation: www.searchenginejournal.com/how-to-use-link-title-attribute-correctly/7687

If page headers can be coded to be an H1 tag vs. an H2 tag, that can help with SEO – you can adjust the CSS to make this change transparent to the user but in the eye of the search engine, it makes the headlines appear more prominently.

Page titles (the actual title configured in the page header and what you see in the browser header) can be further optimized. For instance, "Buyer's Guide | Your Magazine" is OK but adding a keyword in front of "Buyer's Guide" makes it better (just try to avoid reusing a keyword twice if it appears in your brand/publication name, especially if the keyword is competitive).

Image ALT tags are important to utilize because it helps tag your images and enhances their association with your web page/site.

A nice tool that simulates how Google sees your site can be used by going to Google Webmaster Tools and using the "Fetch as Googlebot" process (underneath Diagnostics).

ADDITIONAL RESOURCES

Good resources to learn the latest SEO trends/practices:

- How to Spot Keyword Trends - www.seobook.com/how-spot-keyword-trends
- SEO Book - www.seobook.com
- SEO Chat - www.seochat.com
- WebProNews - www.webpronews.com
- SEOmoz - www.seomoz.org
- TechCrunch - www.techcrunch.com - not as focused but some good articles posted from time to time
- The Best Keywords Tools | Keyword Research and Trends - www.squidoo.com/finding-the-latest-trends
- Search Engine Land - www.searchengineland.com

SUMMARY

There is no surefire way of handling SEO. Using idea similar to investing in stocks, you want to have a 'portfolio' of web sites using varying SEO tactics. For example, you can have an e-commerce storefront with the same products, but you want to use different templates to begin with and also varying SEO strategies. Google's ranking algorithm changes all the time (among other search engines)... so using the analogy of the stock market, one industry (algorithm) might be strong one week but this could slant towards an alternative one the following week. Or, using the example of two companies owned by the same parent company that offer competing products, you can have contests with each, changing certain aspects of the sites and see what works best and what does not work so well and adjust as necessary.

··· ❼ ···
EMAIL MARKETING

Email marketing consists of a number of important focus areas that should all receive equal attention as you build and execute your email marketing campaign/overall email marketing effort.

This form of marketing used to be the most popular form of Internet marketing back in the late 1990's to early-mid 2000's but has since lost traction, in part to more complex spam filters, regulations, increased costs and new marketing channels such as social media.

SELECTING AN EMAIL SERVICE PROVIDER (ESP)

Sending email campaigns through email service providers (ESPs) is popular today because they maintain relationships with Internet Service Providers (ISPs such as AOL, Comcast, etc.) to white-list IP addresses used with their service, building a reputation behind their service. This method is generally more expensive (up-front) but less expensive in the long run as you do not need to deal with any hassles associated with a black-listed IP address or possibly making a one-off honest mistake or a technical glitch happening that renders your email marketing effort illegal (perhaps in the case of a change in personnel, etc.), giving you 'peace of mind.'

ESPs, like auto insurance companies are not all alike and can be segmented into three tiers. The 'A list' is composed of all top-notch companies that are full-staffed and tend to serve Fortune 500 companies and leading/cutting-edge startups such as Groupon, Living Social, etc. They have the best relationships with ISPs and guarantee the highest email delivery rates in the industry. You will definitely 'pay the price' with this tier in light of the higher value but high-volume rates can typically be negotiated. At times, costs can be negotiated below or match your current ESP's expense if you are switching but you may be asked to commit to a longer period of time (i.e. 6 months, 1 year, 2 years, sometimes longer) and you would be committing to a volume on a 'use it or lose it' basis for packages based on the volume of emails sent versus number of people on your list(s). This is not a huge concern however as many times A-level ESPs allow prospective customers to commit to a small period of time, perhaps 3-6 weeks or less to trial the service and get a sense of what volume they require/end up using before committing to a long-term email send 'bucket'. 'B list' ESPs are also an excellent option but may have a smaller staff and/or fewer resources over A list ESPs. As you may have anticipated, this tier is not as expensive but following the 'you get what you pay for' concept, delivery rates may suffer as a result of a slightly reduced effort in maintaining/building relationships with ISPs, investment in the ESP's technology/infrastructure, etc. C-level ESPs are expectantly the low-cost vendors that get the job done but while potentially sacrificing campaign goals, requirements and results. You may be OK with a C-level ESP if you are willing to 'do more with less' (such as emailing more people hoping to get the same results as an A or B level ESP), but the risk of the ESP going out of business or is greater, as is the overall security of your email lists and other data. There is also a real price tag put on any additional marketing push/self-management, either with paying staff and/or less time available creating marketing copy, etc.

Some great US-based ESPs are VerticalResponse, MailChimp, AWeber, ConstantContact and EchoMail, SendGrid (in no particular order). Another great ESP I have worked with, based in the UK is dotMailer, developed by dotDigitalGroup plc. Each has its own advantages and disadvantages but the best one is really whatever works best for your specific budget, list size, perceived/actual email distribution volume, number of publications/lists, regulatory requirements, advanced features such as triggered/automatic email blasts, etc. A simple decision-making tactic I use that may be helpful in digesting the information is to first make an Excel sheet comparing at least three of these ESPs outlining costs and features. Towards the end of this process, creating a simple chart with two columns, one entitled advantages, the other disadvantages for each of your top choices may help define the best choice for your business (the 'winner' having more +'s over -'s).

As you select your ESP, I highly recommend you carefully read their Terms of Service/use agreement(s). If you have more than one brand using the ESP, especially if managed by more than one person/group, you may want to consider creating separate accounts for each brand and registering new domains to use with outbound marketing (i.e. if the domain you typically use for internal and external day-to-day email communication is @alphacompany.com, you may want to use @alphacompanyinfo.com) just in case there is ever an issue with the number of allowed ISP-level complaints going beyond the threshold, any CAN-SPAM compliant concerns raised by the ESP, the domain tied to the email marketing message being blacklisted, etc. These issues can potentially suspend service or permanently revoke future access to an account which is bad enough for one brand but detrimental to an entire organization. In addition, territorial laws/regulations and ESP-level regulations differ. In the UK for instance, it is against the law to email anyone that did not specifically request to receive email communication from your company (i.e. someone signing up to receive a newsletter via your company's web site is OK but emailing someone from a trade show list, even if it is a trade show you attended is not OK). Many ESPs may randomly pull a few email addresses from time to time to test compliance. On the contrary, in the US, this practice is not illegal so long as you provide a way for someone to opt-out of your email and you are otherwise CAN-SPAM compliant. However, it is generally against ESP company policy to follow this practice and some ESPs test compliance to the same extent as UK-based ESPs do to maintain their relationships/white-list status with major ISPs. With this said, some aggressive marketers will disregard US-based ESP policy and gradually introduce new people to a list while emailing the list. Although against policy, they are typically able to stealthily 'go around' this policy so long as they do not exceed allowed thresholds. If they go beyond a threshold, an ESP may try to work with the marketer to weed out non-allowed email addresses, possibly assisting to do some kind of email based opt-in campaign. (The latter is generally frowned upon as well because technically, if no source evidence exists for a valid sign-up, they are technically not allowed in the first place.)

SELF-HOSTED EMAIL MARKETING SOLUTIONS

Although I highly recommend pursuing an ESP for your email marketing delivery, if for some reason you wanted to take a look at self-managed desktop solutions, a few great programs I have used in the past are GroupMail (developed by Infacta), AtomPark's Atomic Mail Sender and Lyris ListManager (on-premises version). The latter has a much higher up-front cost but if you are sending high-volume email in-house and/or the emails require complex configurations, automatic replies/triggers, etc., ListManager is a great solution. You can also build a somewhat custom web-based solution using Drupal and CiviCRM that works great as well but has a slightly high learning curve to put together and train your staff how to use and manage effectively. Either way, the number of outbound email messages is likely capped by your webmail service provider and/or ISP. Gmail for instance caps outbound emails to 500 per 24-hour period. Many ISPs tend to cap outbound emails to roughly 1,000 per 24-hour period or monitor your bandwidth and will give you a call if they notice any suspicious activity. As an aside, a higher bandwidth is involved with sending HTML/multi-part emails over text emails so if you are aiming for high volume in a limited bandwidth allotment, you may want to consider sending plain text emails in a small volume at first and see how that performs. If you need to increase the outbound email cap, you can contact your ISP to see if they can increase that limit for you or you can upgrade from residential to business/commercial plans. (Comcast, for example limits residential accounts to 1,000 emails per day but caps emails at 20,000 per day for "Business Class" accounts.) Sometimes it is cheaper to purchase an SMTP relay package through SMTP.com or a similar SMTP relay service but you may want to investigate all options as pricing and features change from time to time.

Outsourcing your Email Marketing Campaigns

If you wanted to consider outsourcing email marketing in its entirety (from creating templates, list management, sending the emails, review of metrics, etc.), I know of a popular email marketing/solutions company named e-Dialog, located in the Boston, MA metro area that does great work, as does IndustryConnect in New York, NY (the latter having great expertise in the trade show/events industry). You may be able to find a few others via a Google search.

Email Marketing Campaign Reporting

As you review bulk email delivery software/solutions, keep in mind that you will likely want to have access to email campaign performance data. If you are sending email yourself on your own PC/server, you will not have access to the same in-depth reporting as a cloud-based solution offers so you would want to consider subscribing to a tracking service which may run around $50-100/year to begin, depending on level of reporting offered, etc. Alternatively, you can create your own tracking system to collect basic information such as to get a sense/indication of an email's performance from a number of email opens and link clicks. I do not know all the mechanics of what would be involved to setup your own tracking system but believe it would be possible through using an @CSS import and/or placing a 1x1 transparent pixel graphic at the bottom of your email. If someone opts to display graphics on an HTML-formatted email or clicks on a link, a system could capture this information. A simple tracking solution (albeit with more management/manual review required) would be to upload the 1x1 pixel graphic on your public server and append a ?campaign=YYYYMMDDXX value at the end of the image display URL to help you track number of opens (i.e. for January 9, 2012, the campaign stamp could be 2012010901, where the last two digits represent the day's campaign number or code). You could also track link clicks using Google's free URL shortener and tracking service at http://goo.gl/. Due to the amount of extra management involved with building your own simple tracking solution, you will have to weigh the benefits/disadvantages to see if it is worth the extra time/resources. In my opinion, a paid subscription pays for itself and can offer more detailed reporting (i.e. comparing your brand's results with industry results, etc.) and the reports can typically be downloaded in the event you wanted to switch to another provider.

An important item to keep in mind is tracking is not 100% accurate regardless of the type of system you use. If you have ever compared web site metrics together, when Google Analytics is collecting information and your ISP is collecting site metric data from server logs for instance you will know what I mean. Slight inconsistencies may arise between different tracking systems, with accuracy never being precise with a single system due to a number of factors. The first is one system's algorithm for calculating a series of data may be different over another as is their source of the data they are using to make the calculations, comparisons, etc. For example, a click through might be a +1 when someone first clicks on a link or it might only be measured only after a page fully loads, depending on whether the page passes back information to the reporting server (this is rare, but gives you an idea). Open rates cannot be tracked with true plain text emails and can only be tracked for HTML emails if the recipient's email client automatically displays graphics or they manually have the program render the graphics at read time. If links are encoded (required for tracking), the request first needs to go to the email reporting server and then redirects to the destination URL so if the connection is slow or the reporting server is down, there could be problems here as well. Regardless, at the end of the day, you are most concerned about trends (which typically end up being consistent/somewhat accurate) to help you make modifications/improvements to future email blasts and campaigns and relay this to senior management/your team(s).

DESIGNING YOUR EMAIL MESSAGE

As you start to build your email message/campaign, think about what your email message will consist of. The email itself should:

- Be CAN-SPAM compliant. This essentially means:
    - The email subject line and 'friendly from' email address and sender's name cannot be misleading.
    - You must provide for a way for someone to unsubscribe from the email message via an automated method or provide an email address/phone number to receive unsubscribe requests (either method requires you to unsubscribe someone within 10 days).
    - Provide your company's name and physical address and…
    - The email displays a clear warning if the content is unsuitable for minors.
- Be one of three formats: multi-part, plain text or HTML only.
    - An HTML only message displays your standard email marketing message you may be used to receiving (e-newsletters, political messages, product and service marketing, etc.) These are typically graphic-intensive with either all graphics (not recommended due to spam triggers) or a balanced composition of graphics and formatted text. Formatted text messages, even in absence of graphics are still considered HTML messages due to the underlying structure.
    - Plain text messages are non-formatted text messages. The message will not contain any graphics, bold, underlined or italic text. In addition, no text will contain fonts such as Arial, Times New Roman, etc. (if it arrives formatted, that is only due to the default settings configured in the recipient's email program).
    - A multi-part message consists of a plain text and HTML formatted email. The idea behind a multi-part email

message is the device reading the email will automatically display the most appropriate version to the user (i.e. Blackberry phones and devices with small screens may automatically revert to the plain text message and most PCs will display the HTML version). These settings can be overridden (typically only done by advanced technical users or by IT departments) but will be the case with virtually all recipients.

- o It is smart to shuffle the email format from time to time as one email format may work best for X number of recipients on your list while another email format may work better for another segment on the list.
- o Plain text emails, especially those with personalization/merge fields (if you use first names vs. Dear First/Last name), have great results as well. Sales teams can definitely benefit from this format from time to time.

- Feature a clean, professional design. Email response rates/conversions significantly increase if the email looks like it was produced by a talented creative department – in the reader's eyes (subconsciously or consciously), they know time, energy and money have been invested in putting the message together. On the contrary, a message that looks like it was put together quickly with formatting issues, typos and grammar mistakes is not very attractive. With the latter, the reader may be more inclined to assume the sender is only looking to 'get rich quick' and not be in business for the long run (worst case, you may come across as a 'spammer'). You do not need to spend a fortune for a great template or set of templates – many starter templates are provided free of charge by most email service providers (ESPs) which are easy to modify, or you can purchase professional designed templates from sites such as ThemeForest.net, etc. for roughly $10-20/template – a great deal compared to hiring a high-priced designer/consultant. However, with that said, nothing compares to a nice, custom-designed template that closely matches your brand and I highly recommend hiring a professional designer if your budget allows. One item to consider is that sometimes you can get away with making template changes (beyond simple text-based edits) in WYSIWYG (What You See Is What You Get) mode but other times, this may skew the layout and formatting. This is due to a programmatic limitation with many template editors tied to ESP's at the moment. The 'margin of error' as you try to make more complex/layout changes in WYSIWYG mode. A way many less technical editors avoid these issues is learning basic HTML (which is not that difficult as it is just a set of fundamental tags that wrap around content) and you will have more control over your content and may find making edits is faster from the code view over the design/HTML view.

- Portray a greater sense of creativity, differentiating yourself from the competition/other marketers. As some popular phrases encourage you to ("dare to be different" or "break all the rules"), keep in mind many people are used to receiving emails that require one to scroll down to read the entire email. Why not create an email that invites the user to scroll right to read the message for a change? You may receive higher open/response rates this way. Slightly off-topic, but the famous '1984' Apple commercial comes to mind as I write this which may help conceptualize this idea better to help you brainstorm some ideas (video can be found on YouTube).
- Send to a friend / social media sharing options. This helps spread the word about your product/service offering or other material presented in a newsletter, etc.
- Include a view HTML/web friendly option. Sometimes, an email may not render properly and the recipient might want to view it in their web browser.
- Include a printer friendly option. Sometimes people like to print an email out as a physical reminder of something you sent them or maybe they want to read your newsletter offline

and make notes in the margins, etc. This additional option is not mandatory but a 'nice to have'. Not all HTML emails delivered in someone's inbox get printed properly as the email client (desktop or web-based) tends to strip certain components out and some content can get clipped.

- Have an opt-out mechanism that provides more than one unsubscribe option. If you are just starting out and getting to know how email marketing works, you do not need to focus on this one too much but it helps to retain people who unsubscribe from your emails. If you only offer one unsubscribe option, people may unsubscribe on an account basis vs. just from your list, depending on how your ESP handles unsubscribe requests. For this reason, you should program a way for someone to:
  - o Unsubscribe across all brands (not desirable but this option should be provided to the user as a customer service feature, which ultimately saves you money as it is one less email address you would normally be emailing on a frequent basis).
  - o Unsubscribe on a brand-only basis (i.e. a newsletter/publication brand)
  - o Modify email frequency - useful particularly if you email your list on a daily basis (i.e. daily deals, etc.) The recipient may like receiving emails, but may prefer to receive on a less frequent basis. In this case, it is best if you prepare a special weekly or monthly formatted email to allow the reader to catch-up on the email content they missed, versus for example simply sending them the 'daily' version once weekly or monthly.

- Have an email subject line that entices the reader to open the email. While abiding by the CAN-SPAM rules/regulations, you also need to 'mold' a creative subject. Many times if someone receives multiple emails in the day, they might not click on the email so it needs to stand out from the crowd and grab the reader's attention.

- Feature a consistent 'friendly from' name and email address. Sometimes your readers/audience will white-list the email address used to send your newsletter or other communications so that is one key reason to keep it consistent. It also helps your readers associate varying subject lines with an Editor or sales representative for instance, resulting with greater or consistent open rates.

- Have a clear message/incentive that moves your prospective buyer to purchase your product or service. This is called the 'call to action' or value proposition. Without this, you are essentially 'throwing spaghetti at the wall, hoping it will stick' while wasting time and resources. You should also make it easy for someone to respond to the email, including a "Buy Now" or "Register Now" button above and below 'the fold' (roughly the first 1/3-1/2 point of standard emails), in addition to text links with alternate wording that encourages this action. The text links work best if they are cleverly placed so as to avoid the reader viewing it as an advertisement.

- Avoid language that triggers spam flags: words/phrases to avoid. You want to do everything possible to ensure your email gets delivered and read by the end-user. You want to avoid using words such as "free" ("complimentary" is a great alternative) and others such as discount, winner, amazing, etc. – anything you may have seen in prior spam messages. If you are in the pharmaceutical or medical industry for example, you should be especially careful due to the large amount of spam featuring vitamins, anti-aging creams, etc. Many marketers in challenged fields tend to use all graphics in their emails but this is not suggested (unless all of your recipients white list you/your domain) as spammers caught on to this method a while back as a way around words/phrases triggering spam scanners. You should always filter/pass your email through a spam checker and review the score before sending an email message. If between 0-2 points out of the usual 5 point scale (as with SpamAssasin), you may be OK but anything above 2 points is a cause for concern and you should address any suggestions relayed at the end of the scan. Many web sites offer spam check services, some free, others you will need to pay a small fee to use but offer other services that aim to help save time (i.e. one service lets you preview your email message in multiple email clients and webmail services at once which is also useful in testing how your email's design looks). If you use a spam checker, it is important to test both HTML and text versions if you are sending a multi-part email out. If you only test one over the other for a multi-part blast, your result will not be 100% accurate.

- No one wants to be spammed – don't make something look like you are selling something to them – make them want to open the email and continue read the message. If you do your job properly, beyond making the sale, sign-up, etc. a sign of a properly designed and executed campaign is when the recipient replies back and thanks you for the valuable material you sent them or made available at a reduced cost, etc.

If you are managing large campaigns for your company and want to maximize the effectiveness of your email marketing efforts, A/B (multivariate) testing can help. You can either do this manually or use the built-in configurations found in some ESP administrative areas to automate this. Basically, A/B testing lets you compare different subject lines (most common), in addition to the actual email content and/or varying templates. Factors such as open rates and click-throughs are reviewed and compared to help identify the general feel/spirit of what subjects/content/design(s) is/are most effective/appropriate going forward.

List Management

If you are new to email marketing or otherwise want to continue growing your lists, you are in luck as a number of ways to do this exist. The first is you can do an email harvesting/collection effort using a tools such as Atomic Email Hunter or manually copy/pasting emails you find on the Internet. As you collect the emails, you should also collect someone's name and title and the source URL you found the email on (this is useful for targeting records and also good historical information to retain). You may want to consider removing all 'generic' email addresses such as info@, news@, team@, webmaster@, etc. as sending to these addresses typically results with lower open rates. After you are done collecting emails using a harvesting utility, I highly suggest filtering the list with some kind of email verification tool such as Atomic Email Verifier. This process aims to weed out email addresses that are syntactically invalid, removes email addresses with domain names that are no longer registered, etc. A good tool will also remove 'at-risk' emails that may be so-called trap or seed emails – in other words, if you were to send a bulk email message to one of these, your IP and/or domain name will likely get blacklisted and you will be reported as a spammer. This has a chain-reaction as spam filters such as Barracuda Firewall installed at large corporations typically scan these databases or otherwise have access to these lists which can result with permanent blacklist status or cause a few months of headaches trying to get removed from the list – some requiring 'offenders' to pay a fine). Some of the more popular ESPs will help filter at-risk email addresses for you as it helps them maintain their reputation as well but it is always good to do this before uploading a list as best possible to reduce the risk. It does not matter if the email you send is CAN-SPAM compliant as these private blacklist databases operate to reduce global unsolicited email and punish companies that harvest emails on forums and other web pages.

Microsoft Access and Excel are great (and arguably essential) tools for list management, in absence of a comparably powerful in-house system or all-in-one list management tool/service from an outside vendor. Excel is great for easily and quickly removing duplicates on-the-fly (version 2007 above), while Access is great for managing lists without needing to delete/modify the original lists provided. Access can do list comparisons (useful/valuable for 'removing' a suppression list from a master list (or otherwise 'list A' from 'list B' and so-on), 'combining' multiple lists together based on certain criteria, etc.) Access' SQL tool is very powerful but easy to use at the same time, allowing you to visually design queries and modify basic queries from within SQL/code view. Free tools such as those found in the OpenOffice.org suite are 'OK' in my opinion for day-to-day office admin tasks but simply does not cut it when it comes to the stress-free management and powerful features found in the Microsoft Office suite.

EMAIL CAMPAIGN MANAGEMENT

As you plan your email marketing strategy, you may want to consider creating a private Google Calendar (free with any standard Google account or basic Google Apps account) to schedule emails with. This calendar can be shared with others in your organization, so long as they all have a Google account (I suggest this be done through a Google Apps account however so you can control who has access to the calendar and when, in the event someone may leave your organization in the future). Each scheduled 'event' can reflect an email campaign's subject line, list(s) the email needs to be sent to, email format (HTML, plain text or multipart), whether it requires any merge fields, from name/email to use and any other information that would be useful to the person preparing the email. Rescheduling email blasts is very easy with a Google Calendar as well as you need only click and drag to another date if necessary.

CONCLUSION

A wide assortment of free educational material is made available by ESPs on their web sites. I was surprised when I read some of this as it tended to be very comprehensive, essentially being a full online course, expanding on the basic principles relayed here. Some of this may appear to only pertain to their product but conceptually, the process of designing/building emails and other aspects is very similar among other providers. Definitely worth taking a look.

··· **❽** ···
LANDING PAGES

Landing pages are typically used to convert an end-user/recipient of a marketing message/invitation, asking them to complete some sort of action. This can be anything from someone buying a product or service, subscribing to a newsletter (via an opt-in campaign), registering for an online or in-person event, etc.

The landing page needs to be as simple as possible to avoid distracting the consumer. You rarely want to send someone to your regular web site because that typically has various exit points that could potentially defer many people away from your conversion target/goal if they click on site navigation links, etc. As a result, the page should be limited to one page (if you have various content/information to display/relay, you may want to do this by embedding a YouTube video you recorded and/or use a tab panel to help organize all of the data). As soon as someone goes to this page, they should immediately see some sort of clear button that allows them to buy your product/service or other desired action. This button should be 'above the fold' (they should not have to scroll down, no matter what screen resolution they have) and other actionable links to help them convert should be placed within your landing page ad copy and perhaps another button placed at the very bottom of the page to make it easy for them to convert. The page also needs to be professionally designed to make someone want to buy your product/service and the copy needs to be checked for typos/grammatical errors. If you do not have a designer on-staff or the budget to hire a contract/freelance designer, ThemeForest.net has many great templates you can browse through and purchase at low-cost (themeforest.net/category/marketing/landing-pages).

An important take-away about landing pages to consider is the fact the potential buyer/respondent may only look at the page for a few seconds and the decision to buy may have great emphasis/be influenced by the quality of the page's design and how effective your sales pitch is (if they are not already familiar with your brand/product). You want to give them a very short 'elevator speech'/appeal on why they need your product, the various benefits, value to them self/their business, etc. You should also do a price analysis and competitive analysis to make sure you are not over-charging... or charging too little, which may impact the perception of quality. Place yourself in the buyer's shoes and ask yourself if you would buy what you are trying to sell if you were them.

Also, consider the fact that most people read from left to right (versus moving their eyes around too much on the page), so you may want to have all the core information placed in the main content area and then have the 'supporting' information on the right/side column (i.e. awards and testimonials, download link, etc).

Landing pages are typically tied to Google Analytics or other metric tracking service to help identify how successful a campaign performed, comparing factors such as money spent (overall), percentage of people that 'dropped off' and did not complete an order flow, etc.

An example of a good landing page:
marketbold.com/keywordsniperpro

··· ❾ ···
WEB SITE METRICS AND ANALYSIS

Many times, after a site is launched, marketers, project management and other team members like to see how the site performs to identify areas for improvement. A successful site will call for tweaks and improvements from time to time and analytic tools are valuable in this process to meet business goals/objectives. These tools can also be used as a gauge to measure the competitive nature of their web site against their competition.

Google Analytics is the most popular tool used to measure web site metrics today (a free, yet very powerful product). At the core level, analytics tools are used to help marketers identify:

- Pageviews - a measure of the amount of times a page is loaded.
- Visits - an indication of the actual number of visits made to your site. Someone could visit your site one part of the day and return a few hours later and each instance would count as a visit.
- Unique visitors - a measurement that aims to identify all visits made by someone during X time, typically as long as a site/application has a cookie associated with them. This is typically a more accurate measure of how many people actually visited a site.
- Pages/visit - this tracks the number of pages a visitor viewed in his/her time on the site. It is helpful in determining the quality/relevancy of the content on the site. A low number of pages/visit is not necessarily a flag as someone might be looking for something very specific. But you may want to consider doing X, Y, Z to capture their attention to stay longer (i.e. adding a "You might also be interested in..." section or improving the relevancy algorithm/criteria.)

- Average time on site - as the tag suggests, this gives an indication of how long a typical user spends on your web site.
- % bounce rate - percent of those that visit one page of your site and leave (without navigating to other areas of your site).
- % new visits - percent of people who are viewing your site for the first time. This metric, among a few others is designed to give you an idea and may not be 100% accurate as they might have viewed your site before at home and viewing for the first time at work, etc. Following the trends is valuable for this rather than considering actual numbers.
- % return visits - similar to percentage of new visits, this aims to track the number of people who returned to your site.
- Demographics - where people are coming from (geographically) is very valuable to help you understand where you need to advertise, what new languages it might make sense to convert your content to, etc.
- Technologies used - preferably, all devices and web browsers should be supported. But sometimes it makes sense to focus on developing products for the most current technologies or three browser versions down. However, if a large portion of your audience is still using older web browsers or slow computers/network connections, it is important to cater to this crowd as much as possible or you will lose this segment.
- Traffic sources - determining which social networks, search engines, web sites, etc. that referred someone to your site is important. Also quite important is reviewing any keywords/phrases someone typed in Google or another search engine to find your site to further optimize your site. Is a link exchange program working? Is it worth optimizing your site for second or third tier search engines? This information is all useful to pool together and consider in your review.
- Content popularity - helps identify your most popular and less traversed articles/pages. This helps you cater to your audience better, perhaps experimenting with A/B testing to

see what article subject lines work best over others, what authors are more sought out over others, etc.

Web site metric tools also let you drill down on certain data to identify more detailed information or associated data. You can also configure many of these tools to help you understand what paths users are taking through your site (to help streamline the process) and where people might be 'dropping off' a sales flow process to improve areas that might need clarification, more product demonstrations (i.e. 3D product rotations or a zoom-in feature) and perhaps to shorten the flow. Generally speaking, the easier it is for the prospective customer to find what they are looking for and buy it, you will see more sales. Goals can be programmed to assist in this effort, even to track where a newsletter sign-up box and/or supplementary offers would be most effective.

Some other popular data analysis tools include Clicky and Woopra (for real-time data analysis), Piwik (self-hosted open-source software), WebTrends and Coremetrics. Some of these can be quite expensive but you have to do a cost/benefit analysis to determine whether potential extra work or lack of detail with a free version outweighs the extra hard costs.

You also have to consider whether you want a self-hosted web analytics package or a third-party solution. A self-hosted option might make sense if you have a large number of sites and you are a new company with a small marketing budget (Google Analytics limits the number of sites per account) but third party analytics helps you save time managing software upgrades and provides a way for advertisers, investors, potential buyer and others that may have some sort of tie/interest with your company to verify data.

A few other web metric tools are identified in this Inc. Magazine article:
www.inc.com/guides/12/2010/11-best-web-analytics-tools_pagen_3.html

If you ever wanted to dive in on learning how to use Google's basic and advanced Analytics features, they offer a certification program with free public training resources. So you can pick which training modules you want to focus on learning more about and not be obligated to take the certification test (although it is a good certification to have.) More information on this is found at
www.google.com/intl/en/analytics/education.html

... ❿ ...

SOCIAL MEDIA AND NETWORKING

Virtually everyone knows what the top social media/networking sites are, how to setup a profile/page and basic functions. But not everyone knows how to effectively utilize these sites/tools in a marketing/outreach campaign. I'll highlight a few of the more popular social sites/tools and share a few ideas/tactics marketers can use to increase traffic to a site, build a brand, promote a product, service or event or otherwise reach more people vs. traditional email marketing.

Suggestion: If you setup new accounts for a company/organization, I recommend you setup generic accounts for your individual groups/teams. This is important, especially for professions with a high turn-over and even for positions where people might tend to stay longer, etc. – people tend to move on to other opportunities after a few years and if a personal-branded username is setup for an account (which generally you can't change) and start to spend time/resources building a network on this... or worst yet, when someone leaves, they carry that account with them (or have otherwise been using an existing personal account to build their network), all the energy used to build relationships/networks on company time would be lost. So if your company is Company X, you might want to create a CompanyXCEO account for the company CEO to share insight/news with shareholders, etc... a separate marketing account everyone can share and build, a sales account, etc. Just be sure to create regular exports of your contacts in case a team member mistakenly (or worst case intentionally) abuses a social network's policy (i.e. sending too many emails to LinkedIn 1st connections, etc.) Aside from this concern, it is always a good idea to build regular backups anyway, as from my experience, permanent and temporary data loss from cloud-based services is not all that uncommon and lists are also prone to human error. You may want to make a few exceptions for more personal impact when you are building your network so an invitation to join your network/group doesn't come across as spammy... and some groups/networks specifically require people who join them to be an individual vs. a company/organization-branded account.

FACEBOOK

Great for B2C campaigns but whether it is a truly effective tool for B2B campaigns at the moment is up for debate. On one hand, one can say B2B Facebook marketing reaches more people that might be in the industry but as Facebook is more for keeping in touch with one's personal friends, marketing on this platform may not be as effective and depending on marketing frequency, could potentially hurt a promoter's brand. Marketers can setup a Facebook page (which they can setup a vanity URL i.e. facebook.com/vanityurl after 25 Facebook users "Like" their page) which can get great SEO. Another tactic marketers can use is to setup a Facebook group and invite their contacts to join (and promote signing up to join the group on their web site/email newsletters). Facebook allows users to email group members which can have higher open/delivery rates over traditional email marketing, effective so long as a plain text email message works... always good to mix HTML and text emails anyway however.

If you use Firefox and install the Greasemonkey add-on, you can install a number of Facebook enhancements, one being "Facebook Friends Checker"... if you post too many marketing-oriented posts which might be deemed an annoyance to your Facebook Friends, this is a good indicator of that and you can see who removes you as a Facebook Friend to optionally rebuild a relationship with a client.

INTEGRATING FACEBOOK WITH YOUR WEB SITE

To integrate Facebook with your web site, you might want to first read developers.facebook.com/docs/guides/web. You should definitely consider Facebook comments integration for nice viral marketing on a blog/magazine site. Also a "Like" button, "Join our Facebook Page" or

"Join our Facebook Group" works well, as does a Facebook badge illustrating number of likes a post/page has received. For a nice social effect/greater sense of community, you can add a social widget that shows X number of random people who have liked your page (with their photos, if they enabled public display of them) and number of people that have "Liked" the page overall. A Facebook icon promoting your company's page is helpful as well (standard).

TWITTER

Great for B2C and B2B. Twitter posts have been gaining great organic SEO results lately. The site is experiencing some growing pains with frequent outages noted in the past but is getting better. With Twitter, one can leave hash tags to help posts get found in search results, and if they gain enough traction, can be listed as a trending topic at twitter.com. A user can invite their existing contacts to follow them (either via interfacing with Twitter's contact import tool which works with LinkedIn, Gmail, Yahoo, etc.) or creating a comma-separated list of email addresses. The trick here is to get as many of your contacts following you on Twitter as this is another channel you can use to promote your product/service. Some marketers look down on Twitter as not being truly effective but I'd disagree as the tools Twitter offers can boost a marketing campaign considerably if utilized correctly. Like traditional 'offline' marketing, a good marketer considers (where possible/practical) marketing in print, radio, TV ('marketing everywhere') to carry their brand/message forward as much as possible. A mobile phone app allows you and others at your organization to Tweet messages anytime, particularly useful if you are at an industry event and want to post updates while in attendance. The ability exists through 3rd party tools/services to setup automatic scheduled Tweets for peak times (when you may otherwise not be able to manually send, which is also more efficient) and send automatic follow-ups every time someone follows you. You can also manage multiple Twitter accounts through these tools. Some of the more popular ones are HootSuite (web-based program) and

TweetDeck (downloadable program), each essentially offering the same features but you might want to try both out to see which one you might like best. These tools also help you determine who unfollows you, among other features which helps you determine who among your audience might not be interested in your posts and cater your messages accordingly, while also reconnecting with those who unfollow you to rebuild connections, etc.

Using the @ symbol before someone's username (i.e. @username) is used to reply to a tweet... if you want to "retweet" (copy someone else's tweet and give credit), you can do this manually by typing "RT", space and then @username. There is also a new automatic way to retweet on Twitter – see: www.mashable.com/2009/11/21/retweets-how-to. This segment of my Twitter highlight helps you understand to also start a so-called 'Twitter conversation' between one or more people on Twitter.

Considered a courtesy if someone follows you that you follow them back but not required. If you follow someone and they follow you back (or vice versa), this allows you to Direct Message them (a personal email/message on Twitter).

A particularly useful/interesting way to connect with others is the LinkedIn integration with Twitter... if you want to see who you are connected with on LinkedIn (1st connections) with a Twitter account, you can go to www.twitter.com/#!/who_to_follow/import ("Who to Follow" > "Find Friends" tab) and click on the LinkedIn button. This will transfer you to LinkedIn where you can click on "Follow" buttons and also opt to "Unfollow" people if you wish. Being connected with someone on both Twitter and LinkedIn benefits you because it increases exposure to your posts/marketing – what might be missed/overlooked on 1 site might be seen on the other.

Note: Depending on the size of your LinkedIn 1st-degree network and the number of those that have publicized their Twitter account handle with LinkedIn, you may need to manually go through and Follow people over the course of a few days, possibly weeks as Twitter (to deter spammers), sets a daily limit/cap on the number of people you can follow per 24-hour period.

Twitter is a great tool for PR organizations/groups to monitor your reputation and listen to your customers/client base. It also gives sales/marketing an opportunity to see with greater clarity who is interested in/looking for a specific product/service and can follow-up with them... also useful for research and development efforts. The possibilities/implications are virtually endless – some have even successfully used Twitter to land a new job... even working the other way around (a company rescinding a job offer to someone based on a negative Twitter post, as with the famous Cisco dialog):
theconnor: "Cisco just offered me a job! Now I have to weigh the utility of a fatty paycheck against the daily commute to San Jose and hating the work."
To which an Agent of Cisco replied: "@theconnor Who is the hiring manager. I'm sure they would love to know that you will hate the work. We here at Cisco are versed in the web."
(Popkin, 2009)

INTEGRATING YOUR SITE WITH TWITTER

Many different ways from a Twitter badge showing # of Tweets a page/post has to an AJAX widget that, in real-time displays latest Tweets from your account or multiple accounts/hash tags. If your blog/site is setup to automatically Tweet from a new post you created, I recommend you disable this and setup a field in post/page edit optimized for Twitter (allowing you to manually enter a Tweet)... otherwise your post will be cut-off and won't reflect all keywords/phrases/hash tags and you won't be using Twitter to its full advantage. See www.mashable.com/2009/03/30/twitter-badges for some options. Twitter also has a new content "Follow" button you can place on your site – www.mashable.com/2011/05/31/twitter-follow-button. As with Facebook, standard practice is to include a Twitter icon on a site to promote your account.

LINKEDIN

Primarily useful for B2B. Not just a 'job search' or professional networking/contact management tool. Sales/marketing can use LinkedIn as an effective lead generation tool via miscellaneous filters having the ability to target people in geographic areas and by title/rank at a company, while also keeping in touch with contacts. A marketer can send a message to all of their 1st contacts, cycling through 50 people at a time (not recommended, but possible) or alternatively, post a status update (recommended over regularly emailing a marketing message to your 1st contacts). The 1st connection messages you have the ability to send, along with the paid InMail messages you can send all have the ability to reach someone's inbox with a much higher delivery rate/open rate over traditional email marketing (again, if you're OK with sending out a plain text message). Marketers also take advantage of LinkedIn's groups – if you can build a group up to a nice number of group members, you can normally email a good portion of this list once a week (not everyone will elect to receive group messages but most do and by default the option to receive group mail is generally auto-checked). This is another great way to marketing your product/service. Sending email out more than once a week to the sale list can cause higher than normal levels of list fatigue so the 1 week limit shouldn't impact one's marketing objectives. One can build their network by joining up to 50 groups you notice many of the people you want to network with belong to and then inviting them to join your network on the basis of group membership while (recommended) leaving a brief personal message introducing yourself to them. You may have better success networking with people who have the word "LION" next to their name or tagline (means LinkedIn Open Networker) or another group such as TopLinked, Open Networkers, etc. as too many "IDK" (I Don't Know) queries can potentially terminate your account as technically, it is against LinkedIn's policy to invite people to join your network if you don't personally know them. Another way to grow your network is if you can generate a list of contacts exported from Outlook or elsewhere that you personally emailed/otherwise communicated with, you can import these in LinkedIn, determine which ones have a LinkedIn account (or invite them to create one) and invite them to join your network that way as well. If someone is not a group member and you really would like to network with them, you can always remove yourself from a group temporarily (recommend you only do this for the groups that you can join automatically vs. any long-term approval process involved with them) so you can quickly re-join an existing group if you wish. If you run out of invites, you can always request more and LinkedIn will generally provide you with 500 more invitations to use every 30 day period, eventually increasing the amount to 3,000+ provided most people you invite to join your network accepts the invitations (an algorithm LinkedIn uses to determine the likeliness of you actually knowing the people you invite to join your network).

Suggest you enter your Twitter handle with your LinkedIn profile so those on Twitter can find you / potentially follow you.

INTEGRATING LINKEDIN WITH YOUR SITE

Not too many integration options with LinkedIn right now, outside the API but you can add a content "Share" button to the site. The most shared content on the web (shared through this feature) is displayed at the top of the LinkedIn site after one logs in so this gives publishers/developers a nice incentive to implementing this. Might also want to consider advertising a LinkedIn icon that links to your profile and a link that invites people to join your LinkedIn group. (On the latter, I recommend a LinkedIn group be set as open in most cases for SEO benefit but if you are currently in closed membership status and get a high volume of spam messages, may want to weigh the pro's and con's of open vs. closed groups).

If you are interested in becoming an open network on LinkedIn, you may wish to visit open networking sites where you can download lists of open networks/LION's. Many cases, you can download these lists for free and pay only a small fee/subscription to be placed on the lists. A great deal for lead generation in my opinion and I have seen a few networkers setup auto-responses as a means of immediately introducing their business which is a great time-saving idea (if you cannot send a personalized introduction to everyone as your network grows). Here are a few open network sites I found for LinkedIn, with some offering networking lists for Facebook, Google+ and Twitter:

- Invites Welcome - www.inviteswelcome.com
- Open Networkers Alliance - www.opennetworkersalliancelist.com
- TopLinkedin.com - www.toplinked.com

YOUTUBE

A video sharing site useful for B2C and B2B. Some might be surprised with the B2B aspect, but the truth is YouTube is the world's 3rd largest search engine. You can get excellent rankings on some videos submitted to YouTube, depending on various factors (from your username, video title and description, video tags, views, etc.) The SEO benefit applies primarily to YouTube search results and also Google... you may have noticed some videos being displayed at the top of organic search engines and these are from YouTube. YouTube also provides another means for people to find more information about your brand and it never hurts to submit videos there, whether you are a Yoga studio/fitness club, government/military organization, educational facility/organization, etc. – there is always a creative way to submit a video (training video, outreach campaign, preview/sample of a class or program, etc.)

INTEGRATING YOUTUBE WITH YOUR SITE

You have the option to embed videos from YouTube to your site using the embed feature. You have the ability to show similar videos or disable this feature and also have control over the size/colors of the player. Certain web site platforms/modules allow you to automatically feed videos to your site based on parameters you specify which works great for video blogs or if you want to automatically feed a "TV" or video section of your site. Recommend also displaying a YouTube icon to promote your channel.

FLICKR

Another great way for B2C and B2B companies/organizations to market themselves or products/services. Following the idea behind what I mentioned for YouTube above, this provides another channel and allows you to reach more people. At times, since Flickr is primarily recognized for photos, you may need to get a bit creative with regards to what you want to post with your account but this could be anything from a career/Human Resources outreach program, posting team outing photos on the site, hand off of a large ceremonial check for a charity, a photo to illustrate small classroom sizes, hands-on training, instructors providing one on one training to students, etc.

INTEGRATING YOUR SITE WITH FLICKR:

May be best to utilize Flickr's API using a 3rd party/community module/plugin for this. You can also add a Flickr button/icon to your site to promote your Flickr handle.

OTHER SOCIAL MEDIA/NETWORKING CONSIDERATIONS

Many other social media tools/sites to consider (Digg, Delicious, popular niche/industry-specific social media sites, etc.) that should also not get over-looked, but this should provide a good overview of what is possible with some of the more popular ones. You may have noticed these sites/tools are great for client/employee relationship management as well.

Somewhat of a blurry line between social media and SEO, but Google's latest "+1" feature lets users click on a +1 button placed on sites to help identify credible/relevant/quality content. The results of this button reportedly help a site's SEO/influence ranking in Google based on a social 'QC' (quality-check) principle.

Another social media/content sharing integration item you might like to consider would be www.addthis.com or www.addtoany.com which allows you to share content to hundreds of sites/services very easily. Adding a "lifestream" to your site (a collective static or live stream of items pulled from social networking sites) is a creative way to tie your social network updates/content in one place and can also help SEO.

If you're looking to build your own social network using GPL-licensed open source software (PHP/MySQL), I highly recommend Elgg (www.elgg.org). They have a hosted/service option for those that are not techies at the Elgg web site. WordPress' BuddyPress plugin and related components might also be a good alternative. But if you need to create a highly-customized social network, I might suggest creating it from scratch using Drupal (version 6 vs v7 at the moment as many plugins you may need might be more mature/secure at the v6 level). Drupal has a high learning curve but is very secure and reliable with a large (and growing) user base with many developers migrating to this CMS from WordPress, Joomla, DotNetNuke and others.

They key to differentiating yourself from others in social media and to create a really effective social/viral marketing campaign: be creative and have lots of great quality content! Create content/posts that have good 'viral' qualities and value... I'm being intentionally broad so as to not give away all my ideas ;-) and to open the door for your own truly creative thoughts/ideas. A post of course does not need to be controversial in nature to gain instant media attention (as you might see with many celebrity news channels/sources attempt) – it can be anything.

Some more great info on the web:

- 30 Social Media Marketing Tips and Tactics –
  www.oneforty.com/blog/social-media-marketing-tips

SOCIAL MEDIA TRENDS

Interesting Aside: Did you know China currently has the most amount of bloggers than any other country? 42,000,000+ people blog in China according to a report from Universal McCann (www.universalmccann.com). Asia as a whole is also generating the most content for the web than any other geographic area.

Universal McCann International Social Media Research Wave 3 www.slideshare.net/mickstravellin/universal-mccann-international-social-media-research-wave-3?type=powerpoint

··· ⓫ ···
WEBINARS

Webinars are one of the best lead generation tools available to marketers today. From a webinar participant's point of view, these web-based events are personal and stress/pressure-free and allows them to gather free and valuable information that can help them with a business challenge, process, etc.

A good marketer hosting a webinar knows that he/she should never present the material as if it were a sales pitch. Instead, you want the participants to thank you at the end for the information as if you gave them a valuable free consulting session or else you are defeating the purpose and value behind this form of marketing.

A webinar can (and should, where possible) be sponsored by the company delivering the consultative session. The webinar can discuss the value behind the type of product/service you offer but you should never specifically mention the name of what you are trying to sell. This is a stealth marketing approach and the participant will still be able to put two and two together and naturally ask more information about your offering(s) at the question and answer session or via email after the event conclusion.

In summary, webinars are valuable to marketers because the ROI is typically the highest with this form of marketing over others. The participants specifically sign-up to gain something from the event. Although sometimes you may only have 40-50% of those who signed up for the event show up, the small handful that do show up are your potential 'serious buyers' and you can therefore know your time/effort up-selling/cross-selling to this smaller group of people is time well spent. (An aside, you can increase the number of attendees if you send a reminder email to those who signed up 1-2 hours before the event. It is best to host the event around 1-2 PM EST for North America to accommodate most time zones and you can offer alternate dates/times to cover other markets/territories as well.

Sponsors can potentially pay big money for webinars, especially for B2B and niche markets. The sign-ups, especially those who attend the event are 'hot leads.' You could potentially charge per sign-up or per event.

As you create the webinar (GoToMeeting.com is a popular vendor to do this with), make sure you are collecting more than just first name, last name and email. Title, company name, phone, comments, etc. is all valuable information to collect.

At the end of the webinar, you may want to consider sending a follow-up email blast thanking those who attended while including some sort of offer to entice them to sign-up. For non-attendees, you can offer alternate date/time slots if applicable. In addition, you can collect more leads if you upload a copy of the webinar presentation (even if it is just a PowerPoint slide deck with voice-over) to your site. The videos can be uploaded to Vimeo or YouTube if it meets their terms of service/length requirements (YouTube may not be possible if your presentation exceeds 10 minutes but Vimeo could be an option if it is not sales-centric and comes across as more educational). You could restrict access to the videos by hiding them unless someone signs-up/logs in to view. The webinar archive section on your site also helps enhance your site's SEO and value to the reader with more content. It also adds value to any advertisers on your site, increasing visits, pageviews and click-throughs.

AUTOMATED WEBINARS

If you are a small company or otherwise have a small marketing team, setting up an automated webinar process can significantly reduce the amount of time involved with managing a full traditional webinar campaign. You no longer need to physically attend all of your webinars or wake up very early in the morning or defer family plans/dinner late after hours, etc. to accommodate alternate webinar dates/times for other countries/time zones. The only catch is you would need to pre-record a webinar or present an archived version. You do not want to offer the webinar as a 'live' event (because that would not be accurate), but you could still advertise it as a "valuable presentation," etc. and your attendees would still benefit the same way as if they were watching a real live webinar. In fact, depending on the automated webinar software used, they may never notice the difference.

If you wanted to take a look at a presentation on some more benefits behind automated webinars, you may want to take a look at www.evergreenbusinesssystem.com/why-ebs.html. This page and video is heavily marketed but I liked the concept behind the video. My favorite automated webinar product coincidentally happens to be the product advertised at that URL (Evergreen Business System) because it is low-cost and allows you to host the program in-house. It also has some nice features such as the ability to collect leads via a built-in event sign-up/registration form and triggered pay now/register buttons displayed at timed intervals during the presentation (if you wanted to deliver a sales pitch). Great for product, service and event marketing.

Some other good automated webinar solutions are Quick Sales System, Stealth Seminar, Webinar-A-Go-Go, Autopilot Webinars, Presentation Domination and AutoWebinar Player. You may need to pay an annual subscription fee for one of these but with that said, it also removes the potential stress/hassles involved with configuring/hosting yourself, not to name security and accounting for proper resource/server load variances if you plan on hosting multiple events.

SURVEYS

Surveys are an effective method of receiving feedback from your users, whether it to adjust your web site's UI/UX, e-newsletter content/material/layout, get an initial reaction for proposed branding/logo changes, layouts (new or proposed modified site design), feedback from a webinar or in-person event, etc. As an incentive, you might want to offer some kind of award to get more people to participate in the survey – a free download, free list of leads, etc. If you offer an electronic reward, it requires minimal investment and resources for you to manage/maintain as delivery can all be automatic. You can also run a contest where someone wins a free iPad (a popular giveaway today), cash rewards, points, discount card, gift card somewhere popular with general interest/appeal such as Amazon, etc.

Make it short but sweet: a simple one page questionnaire, multiple choice, nothing required. Best if it is anonymous with no IDs attached to the URL. However sometimes it is necessary to have IDs in URL and you thus cannot say it is anonymous because it is linked back to someone's email address. The latter case is if you wanted to follow-up with people who did not respond, responded to certain questions for follow-up responses/detail, etc. through the survey program itself vs. your own email marketing system.

If you need to ask a lot of questions, it is best to break it down to a few pages, but no more than 3-5 pages is recommended so the survey participant retains interest and does not get discouraged as they complete the survey. You should have some sort of survey completion progress meter so the participant has some sense of how much longer they have to complete the survey. The number and complexity/type of questions on each page should be consistent, with say no more than 5-10 short questions per page and no more than 3-5 longer/more complex answer questions per page. If it is an anonymous survey and you are offering a drawing for an award, allow them to enter their information at the end of the survey and communicate this at the beginning and in the invitation email in order for them to be considered for that drawing. Otherwise, there is no way to tie them to their survey results/record unless there is other personally identifiable information/data included (but you may need to manually sift through the results to locate).

A popular and low-cost service used by marketers for surveys is SurveyMonkey. This lets you customize colors, header graphic, etc. per survey/brand yourself (paid version). The free version is available with limited options and no branding options.

QuestionMark is another great easy to use program for surveys with powerful features and doubles as a great online course/orientation platform. As with SurveyMonkey, QuestionMark is hosted in the cloud so does not require any maintenance or involvement from your IT department/consultant.

If you want a nice, comprehensive enterprise-ready solution that can interface with your Salesforce account with ...Clicktools is a great option as well.

··· ⓭ ···

PRESS RELEASES

Novice Internet marketers might consider press releases (aka PR campaigns) to be a thing of the past. However, PR should never be overlooked because it is an important piece of your overall marketing strategy.

Press releases are an excellent way to gain additional SEO value for your site (this is described in more detail in the SEO chapter of this book). They are also excellent tools to increase brand awareness and enhance reputation.

A number of free press release submission sites exist. PitchEngine.com is a popular one but you might want to consider posting on paid PR engine sites to get your message pushed to more sources. From my experience, paid PR submission sites such as PRWeb and PRNewswire can get your press release indexed fairly quickly, sometimes within 24-48 hours and can send valuable traffic to your site. The latter might be attributed to some kind of mechanism in Google's advanced algorithm that might consider paid PR submissions as posing less of a risk for spam content vs. free PR submission sites.

PR SEO is the term used for submitting press releases with the primary goal of increasing traffic to your site. This concept is described in more detail in the SEO/SEM chapter.

··· ⓮ ···
ADVERTISING

The more channels you advertise in, the further you carry your brand's image and message. A good Marketer will tell you advertising online should just be one piece of your overall advertising campaign (beyond snail mail/USPS bulk mail, TV/cable, mobile, radio, magazine advertising, billboards, etc.) Similarly, with all the advertising options available for online advertising, you should consider all, where possible/practical for your brand, industry, budget and workforce (to place, create, modify ads and manage the overall ad campaigns).

Some popular Internet-based advertising channels:

- Adroll - www.adroll.com - An AdRoll campaign could help convert more buyers. This works well for B2C companies as most sites in the AdRoll network are in this area. Basically, when someone visits your site and goes elsewhere on the Internet, a banner ad follows them as they browse the net (if the site is part of the AdRoll network). Many sites are so it can be a valuable component to the overall strategy. The site allows one to set spending limits which helps control that aspect.
- Google AdWords - www.google.com/adwords - Allows you to place a static or animated ads in Google's advertising network (above and to the right of organic Google.com search results and on network sites). This is a pay-per-click (PPC) ad program.
- Skimlinks - www.skimlinks.com - Contextual text advertising. Pinterest reportedly uses Skimlinks as their primary revenue source (www.readwriteweb.com/archives/how_pinterest_is_making_money.php). The links are tied to affiliate programs and the publisher earns money whenever a consumer makes a purchase after visiting a link.

- Text-link-ads - www.text-link-ads.com - Text ad placement on highly-ranked web pages (typically beyond a Google PageRank of 4 or 5. Has a dual purpose of promoting your brand, in addition to gaining SEO value.
- Facebook ads - The "Sponsored" ads you see on the right column of your personal/business Facebook account, in addition to other areas. Facebook, after the US Government likely has the most information about its members and as a result, allows you to target your ads more closely over other avenues (Foursquare comes as a close second).
- Twitter advertising - Allows you to promote your account, hash tags/trends or specific Tweets. More information: business.twitter.com/en/advertise/start
- LinkedIn advertising - Makes sense if you want to promote your business, trade show/industry event, further promote a job, your personal profile or a specific product/service.
- If you are promoting physical goods/services, Groupon and LivingSocial and other deal sites are excellent sources to advertise in. If your audience is primarily composed of Internet marketers, AppSumo.com is another great avenue that emphasizes the promotion of digital goods to this vertical/niche.

TOP THREE NON-PPC WEB ADVERTISING NETWORKS

If you want a more automated approach towards your web site advertising initiative, there are a number of web advertising networks to choose from. For many, Google's popular AdSense program works but it does not necessarily produce the most relevant ads due to the way it works (contextual advertising based). For those that want to veer away from contextual advertising options such as AdSense, Vibrant Media's IntelliTXT or Kontera's ContentLink service, 3 alternatives exist that may actually suit your needs better. These options involve for formal advertising networks serving ads specific to one's target audience/niche.

To learn more about these options, you should visit the following 3 web sites and decide which one may be best suited for your needs. Adify and AdBrite are designed more for consumer oriented web sites while Adroll offers more specific targeting for B2B companies in addition to B2C.

- Adroll - www.adroll.com
- AdBrite - www.adbrite.com
- Adify - www.adify.com

GOOGLE ADWORDS

Google offers a number of promotional coupons from time to time for their AdWords program. There is no real 'catch' with any of these offers, although some codes may only work for new accounts setup through a link so you might want to plan on entering the coupon codes/credits in accordingly (creating the account through the link first and then add the supplementary coupon codes in to increase your promotional credit).

The other item to be aware of is Google does not let someone create a 'cap spending at X amount' setting for an *entire* campaign, only allowing one to cap spending on a *daily* basis. So depending on the competitiveness/geographic area used for the advertising campaign, the daily limit can quickly be reached and if forgotten, Google continues to charge up to that amount every day until the campaign is manually paused/cancelled (can be very expensive but I would always be OK with a task reminder set on a calendar to log in to stop a campaign when my daily spend limit reaches my budgeted amount).

Also, a lesser-known trick that can increase ROI is if an ad is setup to run on network sites. I'd Google keywords/phrases and create a list of URLs that a) rank high and b) feature AdSense ads (Google ads placed on blog sites, etc.) and then type those in the AdWords system. Sometimes a bit more effective vs. advertising on the right-hand column of Google organic results and less expensive.

Retailers tend to use AdWords to promote their own products/services (so long as the phrases/words are not overly competitive as that can convert to an expensive advertising campaign), while also focusing on promoting them in ads that have their product's part number(s) and/or model number(s). The latter is generally not as competitive/costly over promoting a product using common phrases and words.

If you want to learn more about how AdWords works and would be interested in earning certification, Google offers a well-respected certification program to help you master all concepts behind the program, from beginner to advanced topics. More information can be found at www.google.com/adwords/professionals

KONTERA'S CONTENTLINK AD SYSTEM

Functioning similarly to Google's popular AdSense ad serving program, Kontera's ContentLink system places ads within the context of your web pages by automatically linking keywords/phrases to various advertisements.

For example, you may view an article and see a double-underlined phrase and when you point your mouse over the link, a 'bubble' appears (such as the conversational bubbles you see in newspaper comic strips) displaying an ad relevant to that specific phrase. These ads appear in a variety of different formats, embedding text and/or static graphic ads or even dynamic flash video ads. Interestingly enough, ContentLink ads bypass built-in pop-up blockers in at least Microsoft Internet Explorer and Mozilla Firefox so implementing this could prove to be a valuable enhancement to your web site, if practical.

As a pay-per-click program, publishers earn extra income if a user clicks on the ads displayed in the ContentLink ads. Per Kontera's guidelines for new accounts, the program is currently limited to web sites receiving at least 500,000 page impressions per month although they may be willing to waive this guideline on a case-by-case basis.

Once implemented on your web site, you may need to fine-tune the appearance of the ContentLink links appearing within your content. Publishers have the ability to customize the link's color, whether the link is to be single or double underlined and can program filters using span tags associated with a class Kontera defined to prevent ads from appearing in certain areas of a specific web page. Publishers can also adjust the frequency of ContentLink ads, preventing certain keywords/phrases from being attached to ContentLink ads, etc. via an e-mail request to Kontera.

In summary, ContentLink offers yet another web advertising stream for you to use that cleverly embeds advertisements with hyperlinks associated with your web page content. For more information, visit www.kontera.com/default.aspx?id=20 for a full overview of Kontera's contextual advertising solution for publishers.

EARN EXTRA WEB REVENUE WITH GOOGLE ADSENSE FOR CONTENT

Not to be confused with Google AdWords, the Internet giant's service placing ads on Google.com search pages, AdSense (when properly configured) automatically places relevant AdWords advertisements on web pages. The service is open to everyone and Google pays you every time someone clicks on one of their ads on your web site. (Be careful however of testing/clicking on one of these ads placed on your web site as that is considered click-fraud and Google has been known to crack down on these cases, suspending and/or terminating AdSense accounts and voiding any revenue generated from qualified clicks.) In case you may not already be aware, AdSense is a pay-per-click program falling under the contextual advertising area.

I personally have heard of one case where a publisher has made as much as $60,000+/year on AdSense revenue and one even shared at an industry conference his company pulls in $300,000/year on qualified AdSense click-throughs. Although these accounts are unverified, I do not see how this would not be possible per personal experience integrating AdSense on various web sites and watching this revenue grow over time. Bloggers for instance are notorious for using AdSense as their primary source of income, allowing many to function as independent, full time/professional bloggers. Google has published a few interesting case studies on this topic, which may be viewed at www.google.com/adsense/success. You may also be interested in reviewing Google's official AdSense Blog (adsense.blogspot.com). If your site (or sites) pull more than ~50,000 pageviews per month, you may be surprised to see how well this program can perform.

Some optimization may be required for optimum results, such as adjusting the size and placement of the AdSense ads, colors, etc. One negative about these ads is that they presently do not launch a new window when a visitor clicks on them, which pulls them away from your web site. This is not to say however that, with some clever programming (on your site) the links embedded within the AdSense ads can do this. As a result, you may want to consider placing the ads towards the bottom of your web pages or anywhere you feel comfortable allowing your visitor to exit the web site. As one person put it, they looked upon the ads as a way to collect a small tip upon the visitor leaving.

A common misconception with the AdSense for Content ads is that they do not allow the site owner/Webmaster to remove Google's "Advertise on this site" option. This can in fact be removed through the AdSense control panel although it may take anywhere from a few hours to a day or so for this to disappear from current ad placements. You may actually want to consider doing this as Google does not currently pay commission from ads sold through this channel - they simply encourage the use of this as it can potentially display more relevant ads and thus drive click-through revenue higher.

Another misconception is AdSense only drives text ads. While this may be the most popular, Google also allows one to display traditional image ads and even flash video ads if they are relevant to the web page content and if an image ad/flash ad is available for a specific ad size (there are a number of ad sizes available, many corresponding to IAB Standards and Guidelines (universal web ad sizes per www.iab.net/standards/adunits.asp).

You will need to decide whether this program is practical for your site and your site's audience but AdSense has proven to be effective for thousands of Webmasters/e-commerce marketing professionals. Whether you are displaying the ads exclusively or running the ads in the absence of traditional CPM or fixed-priced ads, you may find AdSense for Content a worthwhile pursuit for enhancing revenue from your web site.

If you run a blog or other site, AdSense ads and other contextual and automated network ad placements are a great way to earn extra income as it removes ad contract negotiation, collecting payment, avoiding scenarios where the advertiser does not pay you (Google requires their advertisers to pay up-front), managing ad inventory, etc.

TRADITIONAL 'MANUAL PLACEMENT' ADVERTISING ON THE INTERNET

Many times, it is worthwhile to place ads on your site the 'old fashioned way' (or send your ad to other sites). The amount of time an advertisement runs depends primarily on whether the ad system is programmed to run ads in a specified time period or by number of impressions (CPM). If the ad is text-based and you are participating in a PPC campaign, ads can expire after your daily/weekly/monthly budget is exhausted, or after a specified time frame.

The two most popular advertising systems are OpenX and Google DoubleClick. DoubleClick used to be an expensive solution until Google purchased the technology and integrated/refactored it into their own platform.

If you place ads, be sure to take note of the standard web ad sizes described/illustrated by the Interactive Advertising Bureau (IAB) - www.iab.net/standards/adunits.asp. This will help you create standard ad sizes (to avoid having to regularly recreate new ads) and setup standard ad blocks on your own site(s) that are often used in the online advertising field.

AS A PUBLISHER

You can charge a premium for CPM/time based ads if your site focuses on a specific industry (B2B). It is difficult to charge a premium for B2C web sites.

If your advertiser wants to advertise in an ad block but does not have the proper size ad, it is often beneficial to offer to create the ad for them at no charge if they can provide a sample and a copy of their logo, ad message, etc. I would only suggest doing this for static (no animation) ads unless you are working with a big client/account where it might make sense to 'go the extra mile' as a customer satisfaction effort. However, if it would require significant time to do an ad, do not be afraid to quote the client for the work performed or ask them to work with their ad agency (if applicable) to create an ad that will work with the new ad format.

Make sure you have all ad specs (sizes, formats, display time, CPM allotment, etc.) carefully spelled-out in a contract. Also include information on who is to create/supply the ad and any penalties for missing the ad deadline (i.e. liquidated damages as a result of reserving the space, preventing other paid advertisers to run their ads in that spot). If the ads are to automatically renew or stop after X amount of time, that is good information as well. You basically want to try to think of anything that should be communicated up-front and not be taken for granted, even include when payment is due (i.e. "NET30", etc.) As an aside, some advertisers like to track ads with their own system or regularly replace/update ads. This adds additional time managing their campaign so you have to decide if you are OK with this, limiting updates during their campaign, etc. This can be a challenge if you have a weekly newsletter and the advertiser has more than one ad placement on the issue and other advertisers want to update their ads as well.

As an Advertiser

Do not be afraid to ask for third party stats (shared access to a system such as Google Analytics or previous ad campaign performance in an advertising system). If a publisher wants to charge you an 'arm and a leg' because their site receives 1,000,000+ pageviews a month, that is worth verifying unless it is obvious, as may be the case with a national or regional TV news network or the online version of your local newspaper.

Get everything in writing and ask for regular ad campaign performance reports – once weekly is not unheard of and at times you might want to consider a higher frequency (i.e. the day after sending a newsletter out, a week later and two weeks later). Many times, publishers can configure their ad systems to automatically send a report to you in PDF format and deliver via email.

DIGITAL PUBLICATIONS

A digital edition, sometimes referred to as a digital magazine, ebook or e-magazine is typically a full copy of a print magazine a reader can virtually 'flip' through page-by-page online. They tend to have a linked table of contents and search features for easy navigation and sometimes add interactive features to what would otherwise be static content in the magazine (i.e. advertisements and publisher content may feature a video, 3D interactivity, virtual tours, etc.)

Some digital editions can be downloaded as a low or high-res PDF to allow the reader to keep an archive on their computer or view historical copies on the publisher's web site.

They are important to publishers because it adds extra value to readers and advertisers. The benefit to readers is they can receive the digital version before they receive the print version and the format is a bit different if they prefer the digital edition over the other. Advertisers see additional value as it is another channel they can reach readers with and links/logos go to their web site and sometimes a reader can fill out an order form or request more information directly through the online version. Advertisers typically do not pay extra for their ad to display in this edition because it was already included in the print version. However, they may pay a premium if they want their ad to stand out more or if dynamic options are added (i.e. a pop-up video, lead capture, etc.) Additional advertisements can be placed around the digital edition embed area such as a full banner ad placed above and/or below the publication, tile/skyscraper ads placed to the left or right of the area, pop-up ad displaying on the cover page, interstitial ads, etc.

Digital editions also have great SEO if the software that created the digital format allows the publisher to dump the page text behind the

Flash output as this gets picked up by search engines.

Some publishers do not offer a print version and may just offer the digital edition to save money mailing and producing/printing the print magazine. Others may first 'go digital' and then try a print format once profitable (i.e. as reportedly the case with TheAtlantic.com). Sometimes, as with the case with the Audubon society, they offer more issues (adding another year) if a reader wants to go solely digital with no print version. The benefit here is it saves the company money and gives the reader more for their money, saving clutter, a step towards preserving the environment (less trees used for paper), etc.

An ebook is generally first created in Adobe InDesign or QuarkXPress and exported as a PDF without crop marks, etc. in the gutter. All PDF pages should be in a single file, be high-res and have the same page dimensions. In Adobe Acrobat Professional, all links should be created (via an automated first pass using the link creation tool) and then a manual page-by-page pass to link logos and embedded links in graphics that did not get picked up/generated for some reason. At times, you may need to crop an automatically generated link or adjust URLs (this stage is part of the QA/QC process). You may need to optimize the PDF to embed fonts, etc. Once done, you can import this to the ebook creation web site where it gets converted for you after you enter the title and specify basic/core conversion options. Most times, this information gets saved for you for next time you convert a publication but you might want to manually save just in case to be sure.

Popular low-cost ebook/digital edition creation programs/software are:

- **eMagCreator** - www.emagcreator.com - Publisher and agency options available. Owned license with service fee for upgrades and metrics after the first year.
- **Virtual Paper** - www.myvirtualpaper.com - Upload PDF to site. Can negotiate pay on individual basis or for x number of

issues up front. Roughly $120-140/issue with 4 issues a year. Volume pricing available for high volume.

Zmags and Texterity are also good full-service digital magazine vendors used by the publishing industry if you wanted to outsource the whole process rather than pursuing an in-house solution.

How to Sell Digital Publications

You can potentially make a nice profit from selling digital publications as the process can be fully automated. You do this by writing the publication and then converting it to a PDF and uploading to e-junkie (www.e-junkie.com) or a similar service. This service integrates with your PayPal account, so whenever someone purchases your publication, they instantly receive the PDF and you get paid. You can also set up a landing page and sell through other channels such as ClickBank (www.clickbank.com) and Amazon.com to optimize profit. As a small caveat, if you sell on Amazon.com, make sure your publication is the best it can be, because if it contains errors, buyers will pick up on these and reflect issues such as these in their review (a five-star rating system is prominently displayed beside each listing, which gets updated in real-time).

If you sell digital goods, you might want to consider looking into encryption and copyright protection/monitoring services to help prevent others from sending a copy of your publication to a friend or colleague. These services can be somewhat costly however, especially for independent publishers, so it sometimes helps to have a 'please be honest' message prominently presented at the beginning of your PDF, with contact information provided encouraging others to contact you if they received a free copy without your permission.

Niche daily deal sites sometimes feature digital publications for sale, so that might be another nice avenue for you to offer your product.

Various email list rental services allow you to send your ad/message to millions for only a few hundred dollars, with targeting options provided. Both options are relatively cheap and can greatly enhance your ROI.

Do not be afraid to post an update on LinkedIn, Twitter, Google+ and Facebook, among other areas to further promote your publication, if relevant to your audience. This is useful if you have many followers/connections, even if there is some duplication between the social media channels as someone might frequent one site over others. The more people (and the more times someone) see(s) your ad, the greater the probability your publication will get purchased.

If you sell an ebook, I highly suggest you create a one page 'landing page' with a professional video embedded from YouTube (where possible), along with a JPG of your book cover. You can put together a nice professionally-designed page fairly quickly by purchasing a ready-made template for around $10-20 off ThemeForest.net and other template libraries.

You may want to consider including a free copy of another ebook (or perhaps a small 'special report') with 30 minutes of free email-based consulting time expiring 6 months from the purchase date to encourage more sales. The only caution is sometimes "free" add-ons might reduce the perceived value of your book, so you might want to advertise the collection as being "included" in the cost.

Authors tend to offer a free chapter on a landing page to allow potential buyers to preview the product, so you might want to consider this with your strategy as well.

··· **16** ···
MERGING OR BUYING AN EXISTING BUSINESS

Sometimes it makes sense to merge or buy an existing business versus attempting to clone a business model. This is particularly true if a competitor has a considerably larger customer base, various patents that protect their product/service or any other element that would otherwise conflict with your ability to take your idea to market faster.

If you ever consider purchasing an Internet-based business, a few questions you may wish to ask (or request for review) are:

1. **3rd party traffic analysis (i.e. Google Analytics report, hosted WebTrends report, etc.)**
   3rd party traffic analysis is useful as analytics provided otherwise can potentially be altered. I would ask for a guest login (or have them share access to the 3rd party stats) to review the statistics or if that is not possible, a PDF export of the information you'd like to review. I would recommend data for the past 3 years (2 years minimum) to get a good view on visitor traffic trends... preferably in a month-to-month analysis (individual reports for January, February, March, etc.) Aside from any other info you may find useful, the report should at least contain unique and non-unique visitors, unique and non-unique pageviews, top 25-50 referring web sites, top 50-100 keywords/phrases, average time spent on site, visitor demographic info, pages/visit analysis and percentage of new visits. Percentages of # of a) direct traffic to web site b) search engine traffic and c) referring site traffic is useful as well. You may wish to ask the company if they setup a filter to block internal traffic from accounting on the report.

2. **Financial data** - Perhaps inquire about the site's revenue model/how they make money, financial data from past 3+ years, if they owe money to anyone, how much $$ in cash reserve (if relevant), etc. An important question would be to

determine if they have any existing advertising contracts and determine how many, when they expire and how much $$ is involved with the contract. If they have a paid magazine tied to their brand, do they owe any issues to anyone? Have they been backed by venture firms or do they have any partners with rev-share agreements?

3. **Legal aspects** – Does the company have a history of bankruptcy? Any current/known future legal issues/cases?
4. **Maintainability** - How many people currently maintain the web site? Are they part time/contract, full time? How many hours/week required to maintain?
5. **Technologies** - What programming languages have been used to program the site? What types of databases have been used? Does the company host the site at their location or do they outsource web hosting? If outsourced, is the site hosted on a virtual, semi-dedicated or dedicated server? What are the costs involved with hosting the site? Any obsolete ("legacy") technologies/software associated with the site?
6. **Domains** - What domains are associated with the site, aside from the primary domain? Would you also get the .net and .org equivalent, any domains with typos, plural/non plural equivalent of domain, etc. if applicable? Who are the domains registered to (if a different party is indicated, might be a good idea to inquire why). Also a good idea to see how long a domain has been registered for – the longer the domain has been registered, generally speaking, we see a correlation with the long-term SEO value for the site.
7. **Sub sites/satellites** - Are any smaller "branch" or SEO-optimized web sites associated with the parent web site and if so, would they be part of the deal? (i.e. a manufacturer's parent site showing various categories of items but they may have other web sites that cross link with each other and may focus on specific items such as product x, product y, etc.)
8. **Marketing lists** - Where did they get their lists? How many lists? Of those, how many are opt-in and how many on lists

otherwise? May be good to ask as some email marketing companies won't allow non opt-in lists from being used. What email marketing system do they use? How often do they send email campaigns out for themselves and 3rd parties/partners? Are any of their lists limited use/seeded? (Occurs with purchased/rented lists sometimes)

9. **Market intelligence** - If the company has created surveys, can we review the data? Any other info we can review in this category? (i.e. usability studies, etc.)

10. **Design** – Is the site professionally designed and does it feature an easy to navigate interface?

11. **Content** – How many pages does the site have? Does the site have too much content or too little? Does it have more of a marketing focus versus serving as an information source (with the customer/end-user in mind?) What are your thoughts on format/organization of the content and search features (i.e. location of search)?

12. **Business** – How long has the company been in business?

13. **Search engine rankings** – How do target keywords/phrases rank in Google, Bing/Yahoo and other search engines of interest? Do they rank on page one results? If not, the second result page.

14. **Back-links** – How many sites link to the site(s) you are interested in acquiring? The more links on relevant/industry web sites, the more exposure the site can receive and also provides a potentially higher ranking in Google and other search engines. In Google, you can determine how many back-links exist via a link:___ query.

15. **Spam assessment** – Do the domains and any IPs associated with the web sites check out OK against spam databases? SORBS (www.sorbs.net) is a good resource to start with your review. MX Toolbox.com (www.mxtoolbox.com) and DNSStuff (www.dnsstuff.com) provide additional tools you can use. If your domain/IP queries indicate neither are on a blacklist, this serves as a good indicator marketing blasts sent from the site's

domain name will not get stopped in its tracks – at least from a reported spam standpoint. Of course, you still need to take appropriate precautions in the design of the email (subject line, content, etc.) as this could flag an email message as spam irrespective of a zero blacklist status.

16. **Google PageRank status** – As Google is the #1 search engine, it is important to determine how Google ranks web pages, to further optimize a web site. Google ranks web pages from a score of 0-10, with 10 being the best. The average score for a web page is usually around 3-5.

··· **17** ···

SELLING YOUR BUSINESS

Many entrepreneurs look forward to the day when they can sell their business, or perhaps a particular component of the business. You might be interested in reinvesting your profit with a new idea or maybe your business is not seeing the level of success you were hoping for and want to focus in other areas. Or, maybe you want to retire early. Whichever the case, you may want to consider defining a clear exit plan/strategy in your business plan to help you prepare for this potential milestone.

I like to build sites as modular as possible to leave the door open for a fast sale in the future. The site needs to be a turnkey business so the buyer knows they can quickly get up to speed and you can pass the key on to them within a few days. I might suggest the following practices to prepare you for a potential hand-off:

- When installing a CMS to power your web site, install as a traditional base install, interfacing with its own database. If you do a multi-site/network install, the site will share its database with multiple web sites, which introduces a challenge when you need to break the site and associated files out for third party transfer.
- Hosting a site on a shared web host account is OK, but I might suggest creating a dedicated sub-folder within your account's root for each web site. This makes it easier to transfer files elsewhere if the need arises.
- Try to use well-known software over custom solutions, where possible. The more popular a CMS is for instance, a greater number of developers exists to support the site once transferred to a third party, reducing headaches.
- Create dedicated social media handles/usernames, pages and accounts. This not only helps brand your site, it makes it easier

to turn the keys over to another party vs. making a request to change a personal email address tied to one of the accounts you need to hand over (to name one example).

- Google Apps offers a standard (free) account where you can have all of your brand's email hosted from. I might suggest you set up accounts or aliases for admin@, info@ and domains@. Again, if all of your businesses email is stored in a dedicated company email account, it makes it easier to transfer the emails to another party, providing for a more seamless transfer.

- It helps to store all domains in one domain name portfolio, such as GoDaddy. In order to transfer a domain to another party, you cannot have changed the contact/registration details such as primary account email or address in the past 60 days, which is an important piece to keep in mind. Worst case, you can always change the nameservers temporarily, then work with the domain registrar to see if they can make an exception... or try pushing the domain to another account within the same registrar (possible to do with GoDaddy).

- Document all modifications to a pre-fabricated solution (i.e. a commercial WordPress theme/plugin). Preferably, all theme hacks should be done as a child theme so you can easily update the parent the developer provides future theme updates/enhancements.

- Documenting workflow and special processes is good practice so you can be prepared to demo your product on-demand.

In a contract between you and the buyer, you may want to consider factoring in X number of hours between period A and period B, where you will offer to work as a consultant to assist with the hand-off and also when you will perform these consulting services. The latter is key, especially if you work full time during the day as this sets expectations. By expressing the number of hours you will be available to assist with the hand-off, this helps reduce any conflicts and incorrect assumptions attributed to the sale.

You may be interested to learn good ways to sell your web site, product or service. Flippa (www.flippa.com) is a popular site for this and eBay (www.ebay.com) works just as well. But, it appears you may be able to earn more at Flippa with the dedicated focus on buying and selling web sites. When you list your site, you should list all information you can think of (with documentation provided, where possible) that might be useful towards grabbing the interest of prospective buyers. Flippa provides a template you can start from, where you can answer their own standard questions, but you can also provide some additional detail.

I have also seen people attempt to sell their business on Craigslist (www.craigslist.org) and even network with others in a particular industry to see who might be interested, if they do not want to publically advertise their business is for sale. You can also try to connect with a broker to sell your business (a few I can think of off-hand would be W.B. Grimes & Co. – www.mediamergers.com and also Kamen & Co Group Services – www.kamengroup.com. Finally, do not be afraid to pitch your idea directly to business executives/decision makers that might be interested. This method is actually preferred as you do not need to split a cut with a broker or digital marketplace.

··· ⑱ ···
Conclusion

Of the various concepts shared in this book, the important take-away is the fact none of the methods should be considered more valuable over others, from an implementation standpoint. Of course, one channel, such as social media (in some instances) might send more traffic to your site over other methods and you might be enticed to stop focusing on other marketing channels. But, to use an analogy, if we consider a professional racing team, the driver is no more important than his support staff on the sidelines, particularly when he or she needs to refuel, replace a tire and so on. With this in mind, email marketing, social media, webinars, SEO and other e-marketing components all serve as equally important pieces of the overall marketing campaign.

With this said however, it is perfectly OK after trial and error or previous experience to place more focus in a particular area over others if you find one channel to be more effective (i.e. in that it might send more qualified leads, introduce greater ROI from your advertising budget and so on). But the point I am trying to make here is if you completely rule out a particular channel, your campaign may not be operating at its fullest capacity. It is a balance game you have to play (assigning a percent of focus to various channels and evaluating whether these percentages need to be adjusted as the campaign progresses) to ensure your campaign gains proper momentum, while considering time/resources available.

As you grow your business, consider it is always best to grow wealth organically whenever possible as this allows you to control the reigns, as opposed to growing your business faster with venture capital support. It also helps ensure your business is more secure and has a solid base and cash flow in a sub-par economy.

You might want to weigh the pros and cons of growing a business faster with investor support because that can still be very lucrative. Consider the case with Facebook for instance and how quickly they were able to reach critical mass with the appropriate investor backing.

REFERENCES

Cockrum, J. (2011). *Free marketing 101 low and no-cost ways to grow your business offline & off.* John Wiley & Sons, Inc.: Hoboken, NJ.

Karbasfrooshan, A. (2012, Feb. 4). Mark Zuckerberg's 6 ingredients for success. *TechCrunch.* Retrieved from http://techcrunch.com/2012/02/04/mark-zuckerbergs-6-ingredients-for-success/

Popkin, H.A.S. (2009, Mar. 3). Twitter gets you fired in 140 characters or less: The 'it' social networking tool of the hour streamlines your humiliation. *MSNBC.com.* Retrieved from http://www.msnbc.msn.com/id/29796962/ns/technology_and_science-tech_and_gadgets/t/twitter-gets-you-fired-characters-or-less/

Wauters, R. (2011, Dec. 7). Pin down the Pinterest clones. *TechCrunch.* Retrieved from http://techcrunch.com/2011/12/07/pin-down-the-pinterest-clones/

ABOUT THE AUTHOR

Curtis Carmichael has been designing, developing and marketing web sites since 1996. He is author of the popular e-book, Creating Intuitive Web Sites (1999, www.creatingintuitivewebsites.com) and has been recognized by USA Today ("Hot Site" award), Southwestern Bell ("Yours Drools" design award) and MonadNet (Blue Ribbon) for web design/development excellence.

Over the years, Curtis has successfully built and project-managed various engaging Internet communities on the web and high-performing e-commerce sites. He drove valuable traffic to web sites, increasing online publication readership/community participation and goals/conversions. Curtis' unique interpretation of web site/email campaign metrics, survey data has helped plan and execute effective e-marketing strategy.

Curtis holds a self-designed BS in Web Management and Internet Commerce and an English minor from Plymouth State University. Passionate about the technology powering today's Internet marketing tools and solutions, he is currently pursuing an MS in Information Technology at Southern New Hampshire University. He lives in Milford, New Hampshire.

www.ingramcontent.com/pod-product-compliance
Lightning Source LLC
Chambersburg PA
CBHW051539170526
45165CB00002B/803